S·H·I·P·S

Written by
Richard Humble

CLB

Colour Library Books

ACKNOWLEDGEMENTS

Illustrated by
Julian Baker, John Batchelor, Bob Corley, Anthony
Cowland, John Dunne, Dave Fisher, Terry Hadler,
Christian Hook, Graham Humphreys, Steve Lach,
Ian Lowe, Brian McIntyre, Ernest Nisbet, Steve Noon,
Darren Pattenden, Tony Smith, Roger Stewart,
Sean Wilkinson

*The Publishers would also like to thank the following for
their assistance*
Cutty Sark Museum
French Naval Public Relations Office
French Embassy – Defence and Naval Attaché, London
Marine Nationale
Queen Mary Archives

CLB 4437

This edition published in 1995 by
Colour Library Books Ltd.
Godalming Business Centre
Woolsack Way
Godalming
Surrey GU7 1XW

Planned and produced by
Andromeda Oxford Limited
11-15 The Vineyard
Abingdon
Oxon OX14 3PX

ISBN 1-85833-477-2

Printed by Graphicom, Italy

Contents

What is a ship?

Number "9"
Number "4"

Number "9"

Number "4"

"About to set sail"

FLAGS

For hundreds of years ships have flown flags to identify themselves and to send messages to other ships. Every flag has its own meaning.

Ships have carried people and their goods across the seas and oceans of the world since the dawn of history. Even in the modern age of air and space travel, ships remain as vital to world trade and transport as ever. As well as cargo and passenger-carrying ships, fighting warships have always been needed to control the world's sea-trading routes. Since the days of Ancient Egypt, Greece and Rome, the sea power provided by ships has built and pulled down empires around the world. This book describes every important stage in the development of the ship from earliest times. Because many of these ships were later modified, we often show more than one version to show the variety of designs that were available.

WHO'S WHO

There were about 850 officers and crew aboard an eighteenth-century battleship.

1. Captain
2. Lieutenant
3. Midshipman
4. Seaman
5. Gunner
6. Powderboy

OAR AND SAIL

From about 2500 BC to the 1500s AD, both oars and sails were used for driving ships. The ship below is a Greek trireme of about 500 BC.

Yard supporting sail

Stern

Tiller connecting steering oars

Rowers

Deck

Bow

Ram

Oars

AGE OF THE FIGHTING SAIL

A three-decked wooden sailing battleship, armed with up to 100 guns or more, was the most powerful of all warships from about 1630 to 1850. The picture on the right identifies the main masts and some of the sails used to rig this type of ship.

Mainmast

Foremast

Jib

Bowsprit

Spritsail

Keel

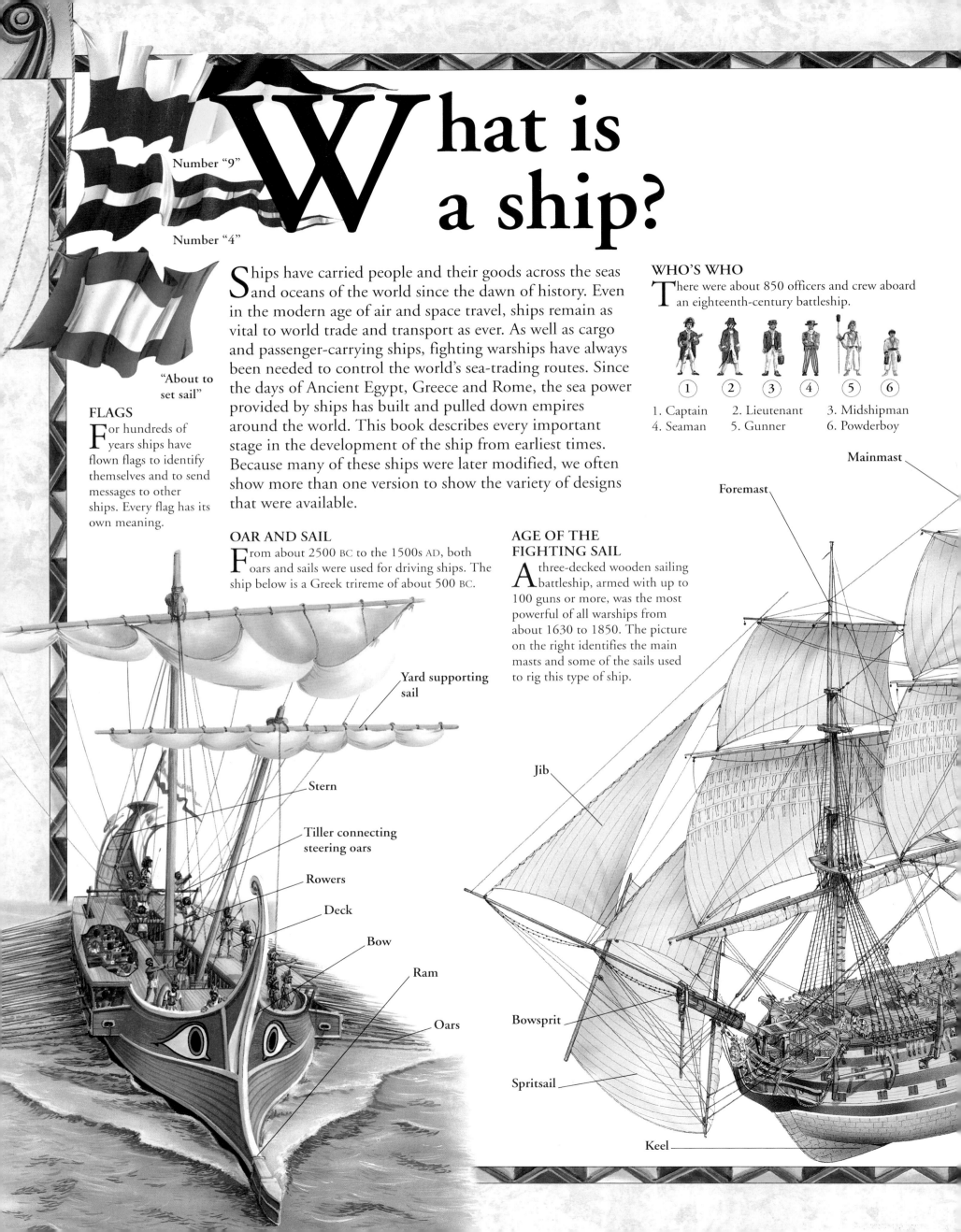

LUXURY AFLOAT

Modern passenger liners have luxury cabins, cinemas, restaurants, swimming pools, and playrooms for children. Safety is also important. For most of their history, ships were highly dangerous to sail in. "Lifeboats for all on board" has only been compulsory since the liner *Titanic* was sunk by an iceberg in 1912, with 1,498 crew and passengers drowned.

Streamlined funnel

Lifeboats

Bridge

Passenger saloon

Rudder

Propeller

Fin to stop ship rolling

THE SHIP'S CREW

A modern ship's "complement" (officers and crew) includes people with many different skills: navigators, computer operators, engine-room mechanics and, of course, a good cook!

① ② ③ ④ ⑤ ⑥

1. Captain   2. Navigator   3. Radio operator
4. Nurse   5. Mechanic   6. Cook

Mizzenmast

HOW A SHIP WORKS

A ship's hull pushes away, or displaces, a weight of water equal to its own weight. Trying to return to its original position, the displaced water pushes the ship up. The picture on the right shows how this allows a ship to float.

Air pressure

Water pressure

PROPULSION

The angled blades of the ship's propeller make the propeller screw its way forward, pushing the ship in front of it.

Some modern high-speed ferries use jet propulsion, sucking in seawater and driving it out in a high-speed water jet.

Stern windows

Amidships

A-port (left)

A-starboard (right)

STEERING

The hinged rudder at the ship's stern is attached to the wheel or tiller. If the helmsman pushes the tiller to the left (port), the rudder and bow move to the right (starboard). If he wants the ship to go to the right, he moves the tiller to the left.

TACKING AGAINST THE WIND

During the age of sail, arrangements of sails were developed that made it possible to sail "close to the wind". By turning or tacking from side to side, a ship could progress without relying on winds from behind.

Gun decks

Stores in lower holds

Hull

7

Development and uses of ships

Down the centuries, ships have changed human destiny again and again. They have carried people in search of new lands in which to live and new markets from which to profit through trade. Side by side with the development of merchant ships, warships have defended trade and conquered enemy fleets. Even in the space age, nearly 5,000 years since the first recorded ships put to sea, ships are still carrying the world's heaviest cargoes and offering passengers luxurious conditions for long-distance travel.

DEVELOPMENT

Designers have constantly looked for ways of improving ships. From single sails to diesel engines, ships have become safer, more comfortable and faster.

HULL DESIGN

For nearly 5,000 years, hulls were built of wood. At first people hollowed out trees. Later, they fixed planks together, overlapping them (clinker) and then laying them side by side (carvel). In the Industrial Revolution, iron and steel were utilised. Today, ships are constructed from materials such as GRP (glass-reinforced plastic).

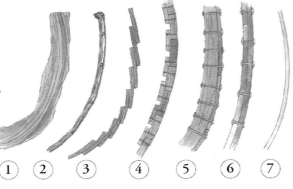

1. Wooden dug-out
2. Pegged planks
3. Clinker style
4. Carvel style
5. Ironclad
6. Riveted steel plates
7. GRP

NAVIGATIONAL INSTRUMENTS

Early navigational aids measured the ship's course and its position north or south of the equator by measuring the angle between the Sun or stars and the ship. Examples are the astrolabe and the sextant. Today, people use electronics, computers and satellite technology.

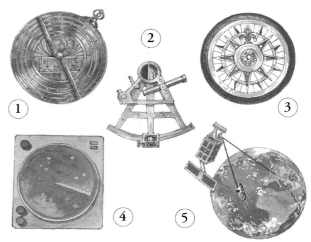

1. Astrolabe
2. Sextant
3. Compass
4. Radar
5. Satellite navigation

SAILS DEVELOP

The Egyptians drove their ships, such as the "round" ship, with a single square sail. This was the only sort of sail used until the Middle Ages, when traders adopted the designs of sails on Chinese junks and Arab dhows. By the seventeenth century, ships had many masts and sails.

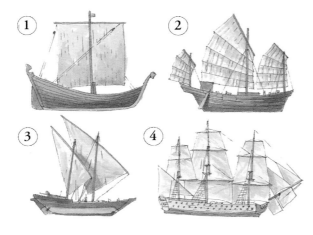

1. "Round" ship
2. Chinese junk
3. Arab dhow
4. Ship of the line

PROPULSION

In the nineteenth century, steam power freed ships from the uncertainties of wind, tides and currents. First came side paddlewheels. In the middle of the century, they were superseded by the more efficient stern screw propeller. The latest high-speed drive is the water jet.

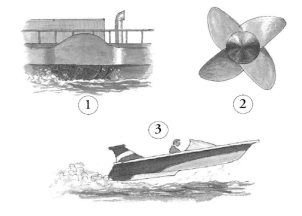

1. Side paddlewheel
2. Screw propeller
3. Water jet

SHIPS DOWN THE AGES

The most dramatic changes in the design of both trading ships and warships have taken place in the last 200 years. From the third millenium BC until the beginning of the nineteenth century AD, ships were powered only by oar or sail.

3000 BC: First known ship: Egyptian reed boat.

1180 BC: First known war ship: Egyptian war galley.

AD 150: Roman merchant ship: used for trading throughout the empire.

850: Viking longship: development of clinker-style hull.

1490: Spanish caravel: development of carvel-style hull, with three masts.

USES

Ships are used in a variety of human activities: trade, warfare, emigration, exploration, scientific research, leisure and tourism, life-saving, fishing – even agriculture. The pictures below illustrate some of the different activities in which ships are involved.

TRADE AND COMMERCE

Ships play a vital part in a nation's ability to trade by importing or exporting a variety of cargoes. Cargo ships include tankers that carry crude oil and container ships that carry solid goods. Ships are also used for obtaining resources from the sea. The picture to the right shows a trawler. It drags its nets through the sea to trap fish.

PASSENGER SHIPS

Different types of ship exist to transport people across the seaways. Ferries, hovercraft and hydrofoils enable passengers to cross seas quickly and efficiently taking their own transport with them. Passenger liners were developed at the end of the last century as one of the most luxurious forms of travel ever known. They are no longer able to compete with jet airliners for speed or price, although ocean liners, shown above, are used for luxury holidays.

MILITARY SHIPS

Military ships can be used as a base for troops and weapons. For example, aircraft carriers provide a fully equipped air base. Military ships are also used for attacking enemy targets. For example, ships such as the French destroyer *Tourville*, shown above, carry guided missiles.

RESCUE SHIPS

Each maritime nation has its own rescue service, and lifeboats play an essential part of this. The picture to the left shows a lifeboat setting out to rescue passengers and crew from a shipping disaster. The lifeboat is launched down a slipway from the lifeboat station into the sea. It uses radar to find the ship in distress.

1570-1620: Development of broadside-firing galleon: emerged as leading warship.

1802: Scottish *Charlotte Dundas*: first working steamship.

1859: Development of ironclads: the *Monitor* (launched 1862) introduced rotating armoured turrets.

1897: British *Turbinia*: first ship with turbine engines.

1906: *Dreadnought* battleship: carried ten heavy guns, transforming battleship design.

1923: First aircraft carriers enter service: British *Hermes* is one of these.

1920s and 1930s: Development of luxury liners: *Queen Mary* (launched 1934) was the largest of these.

1960s: Development of guided-missile warships.

1990: *Hoverspeed Great Britain*: world's largest multi-hull jet ferry.

Egyptian warship

Ancient Egypt was the world's first sea power, building cargo ships for trade and fighting ships for war. Egypt's first sailing ships were built of papyrus reeds, but by 2500 BC Egypt was building elegant river boats and ships of cedar wood imported from Lebanon. The world's oldest surviving ship (about 2500 BC) is the cedar-built funeral barge of Pharaoh Cheops, builder of the Great Pyramid. Defeating the invading "Sea Peoples" with a fleet of war galleys, shown below, Pharaoh Ramses III won the first known sea battle in about 1180 BC. The pictures of the battle on the walls of Ramses III's temple at Medinet Habu show that it was won not only by the ramming attacks of the Egyptians but also by hand-to-hand fighting to board and capture enemy ships. This would remain an important part of naval warfare for the next 3,000 years, until long-range guns and explosive shells came into use in the nineteenth century.

REED SHIPS

Papyrus reeds, growing beside the River Nile, provided pith for Ancient Egyptian paper-making. When lashed together in tight bundles, papyrus also provided the world's first sea-going sailing ships. These were built over 5,000 years ago.

WEAPONS

On both land and sea, the main Egyptian weapons were bows and arrows for long-range fire, javelins, war clubs, swords and maces, and light battle-axes made of bronze.

BUILDING THE HULL

Egyptian builders constructed hulls by pegging together short lengths of plank. Crossbeams ran across the hulls. Decking planks were laid on the crossbeams and the sailors and teams of rowers lived and worked above these.

Steering oar

Archers firing at enemy ship

Mast backstay

CAULKING THE SEAMS

The joints, or seams, between the outer planks were caulked, or made water-tight, by packing oiled papyrus reeds into them.

Masthead look-out post

Sail "brailed" up to yard

Mast forestay (broken)

Single fixed mast

Single sail
The ship could not be steered into a headwind.

Rowing benches
These were protected by raised side-planking.

Single oar
A large oar steered the ship.

An Egyptian war galley of this type, rowing 12 oars a side, was probably about 21m long from the tip of the ram to the stern. Apart from its crew of 24 rowers it could have carried about 20 archers and soldiers.

Bronze-covered ram
For attacking enemy ships.

THE FIRST KNOWN NAVAL BATTLE

After the funeral barge of Pharaoh Cheops was carefully taken to pieces and buried with him for use in the afterlife, over 1,300 years passed before the Egyptians recorded their first victory in a battle at sea. The memorial temple of Ramses III at Medinet Habu shows detailed pictures of the battle, with the war galleys of Egypt defeating the fleet of the "Sea Peoples". The battle was fought off the mouth of the River Nile. The Egyptians won it by ramming and sinking some of the enemy ships and capturing others by boarding them with soldiers.

THE DEADLY RAM

The ram was a forward-jutting extension of the ship's keel, usually armoured with a heavy bronze cap in the shape of an animal's head.

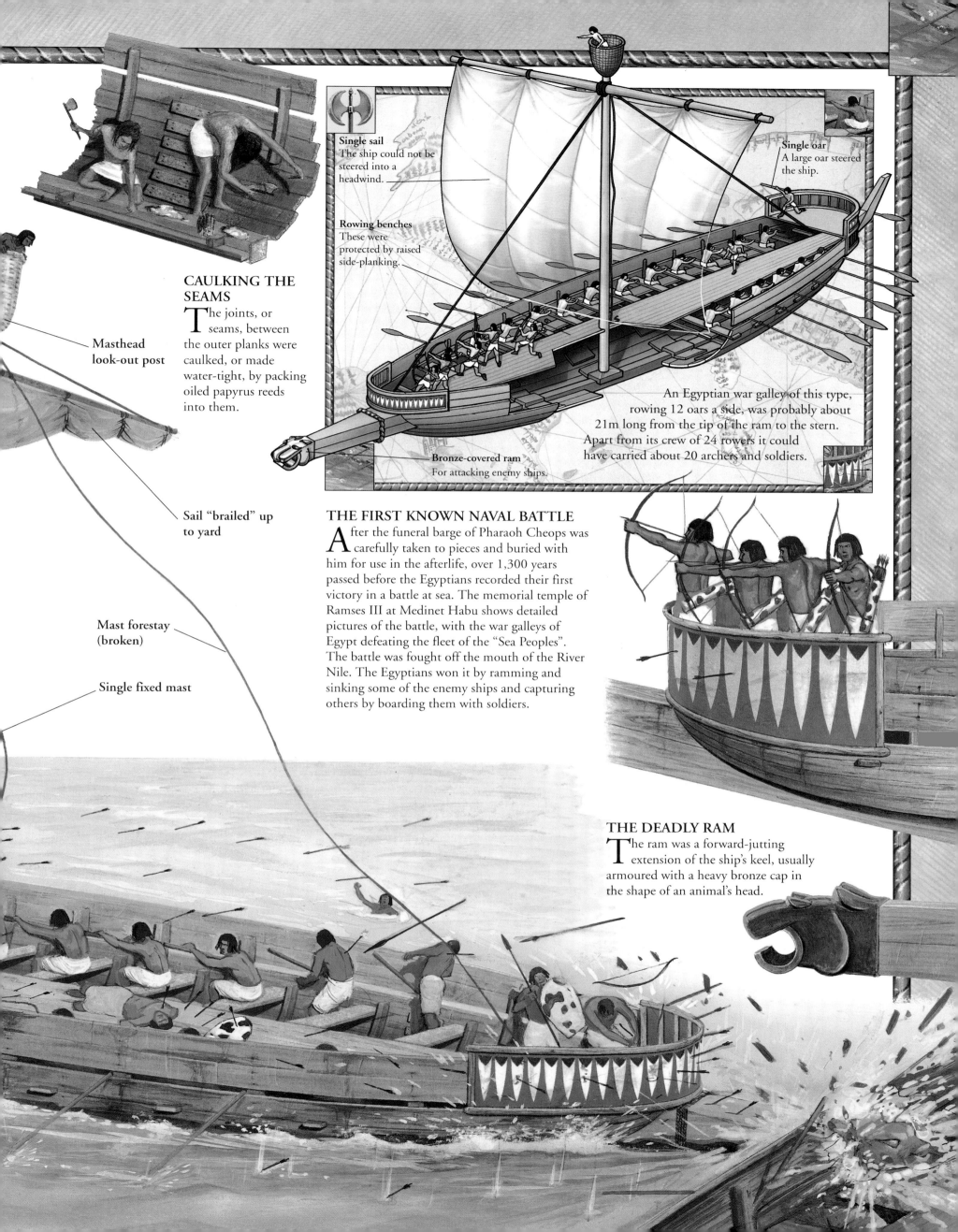

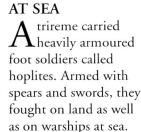

Greek trireme

The Ancient Greeks perfected the war galley with their trireme, which means "three oars". During Egypt's decline, and eventual conquest by Persia in 525 BC, the Phoenicians rose as a new sea power. They introduced the bireme, which had two banks of oars on each side instead of the one bank used by the Egyptians. By 500 BC the Greeks had added a third bank of oars and created a faster, deadly naval weapon.

Triremes put to sea under sail, and often cruised hundreds of kilometres before sighting the enemy. The mast and sail would then be lowered, and rowers took over so that the trireme could ram enemy ships and sink them. The trireme fleets of Athens and Sparta smashed Persia's invasion of Greece in 480 BC. Over 200 Persian ships were lost in exchange for less than 40 Greek ones. Later, in the Peloponnesian War between Athens and Sparta (431-404 BC), there were many battles between trireme fleets. Spartan triremes claimed the final sea victory.

ROWING ON THREE LEVELS

Scholars argued for hundreds of years over how triremes were actually rowed. It was not until a replica trireme was built in the 1980s, with the help of computer design, that the mystery was solved. The trireme was rowed by 170 men, 85 on each side. The oars of the 31 *thranites* on the top bank were carried clear of the lower two banks by an outrigger extension from the ship's side. Below them were 27 *zygites* of the middle bank and 27 *thalamites* of the bottom bank.

"All-seeing eye"

WARRIORS AT SEA

A trireme carried heavily armoured foot soldiers called hoplites. Armed with spears and swords, they fought on land as well as on warships at sea.

"ALL-SEEING EYE"

Above the bronze-capped ram, the forepost swept up in an elegant curve. The bow was painted with an "all-seeing eye", one of the oldest good-luck charms in the history of seafaring. The eye was supposed to guide the ship on its way and bring it safely back to harbour. It is shown in paintings of Ancient Egyptian ships of about 2400 BC, and is still carried by the fishing boats of many nations today.

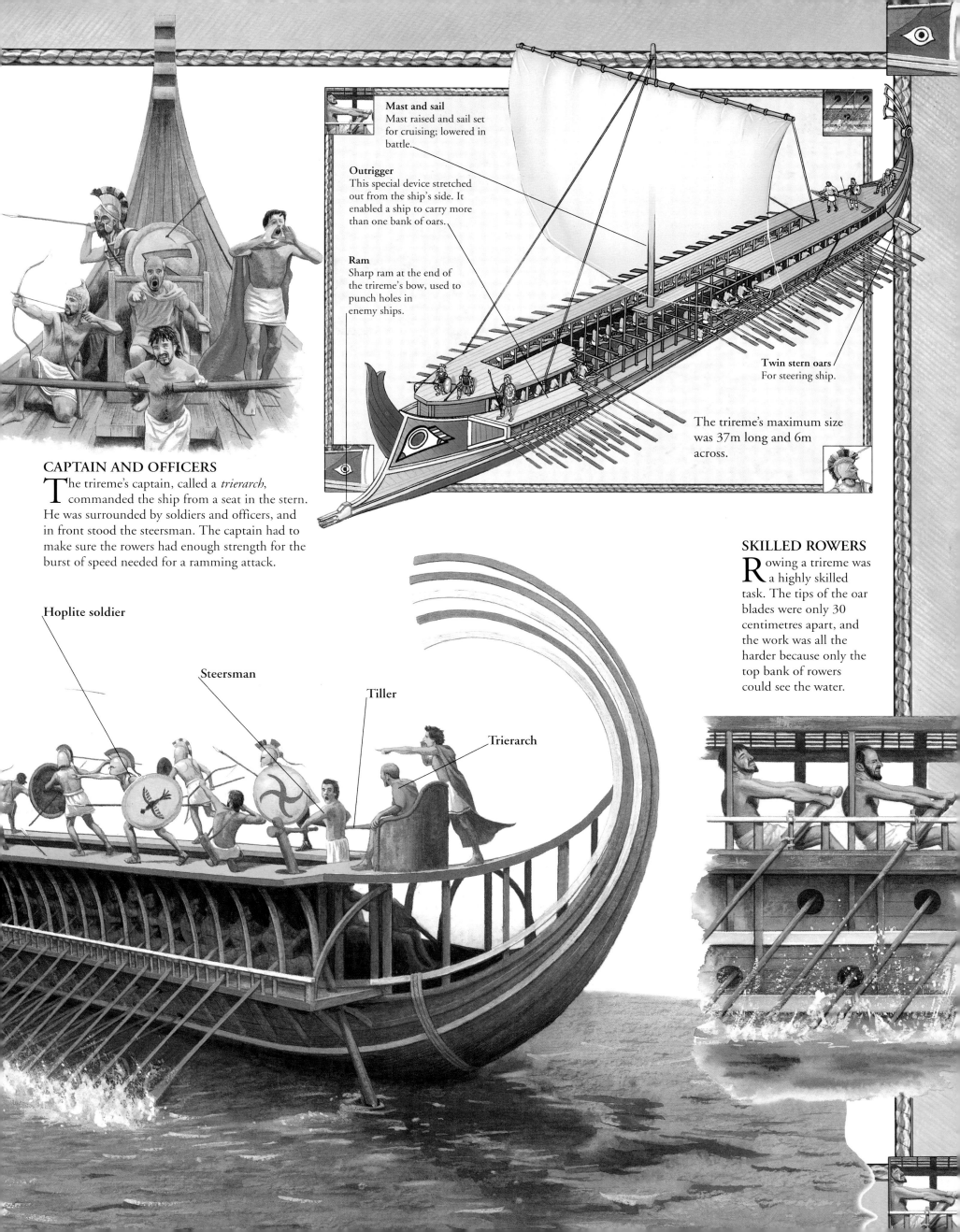

Mast and sail
Mast raised and sail set for cruising; lowered in battle.

Outrigger
This special device stretched out from the ship's side. It enabled a ship to carry more than one bank of oars.

Ram
Sharp ram at the end of the trireme's bow, used to punch holes in enemy ships.

Twin stern oars
For steering ship.

The trireme's maximum size was 37m long and 6m across.

CAPTAIN AND OFFICERS
The trireme's captain, called a *trierarch*, commanded the ship from a seat in the stern. He was surrounded by soldiers and officers, and in front stood the steersman. The captain had to make sure the rowers had enough strength for the burst of speed needed for a ramming attack.

Hoplite soldier

Steersman

Tiller

Trierarch

SKILLED ROWERS
Rowing a trireme was a highly skilled task. The tips of the oar blades were only 30 centimetres apart, and the work was all the harder because only the top bank of rowers could see the water.

Roman merchant ship

" The crew was like an army. They told me she could carry enough grain to satisfy every mouth in Athens for a whole year. And the whole fortune of the ship is in the hands of a little old man who moves the great rudders with a tiller no thicker than a stick."
Lucian

The Greek writer Lucian wrote the above words in about AD 150. He was describing a Roman merchant ship at the port of Athens, then part of the Roman empire. These ships were tough and seaworthy. They carried a wide range of cargo, and the biggest were fitted with passenger cabins in the stern. The cabins could hold more than 250 people, and these were often prisoners or slaves, shackled and crammed together with no regard for their comfort. Since the ships rarely sailed during the stormy winter months, the crew usually slept on deck.

STERNPOST

At the stern of Roman merchant ships, the tall, curving sternpost was topped by a graceful swan's or goose's head. Like the carved figureheads on ships of later centuries, it was painted and gilded.

ROMAN EMPIRE

Rome's empire, shown in orange on the map on the left, depended on trade by sea. Merchant fleets cruised the Mediterranean Sea, sailed along the Atlantic coast of Spain and France, and sailed across the English Channel.

SPREADING THE PLAGUE

Rats often swarmed in the cargo holds of Roman ships carrying grain. The rats carried the plague and helped to spread the disease. It swept across the Roman empire from the Middle East in AD 166.

Mainmast

Spritsail

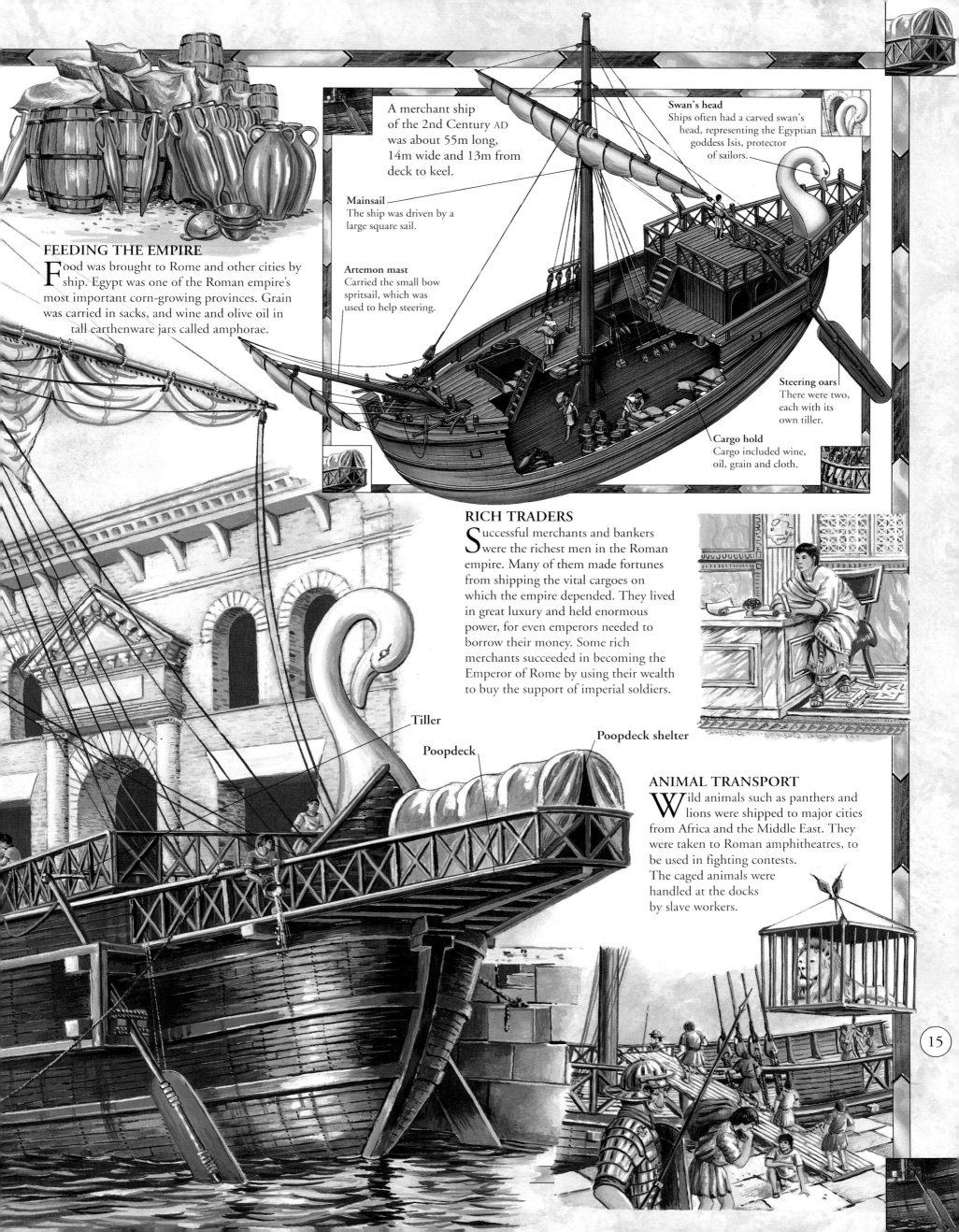

FEEDING THE EMPIRE

Food was brought to Rome and other cities by ship. Egypt was one of the Roman empire's most important corn-growing provinces. Grain was carried in sacks, and wine and olive oil in tall earthenware jars called amphorae.

A merchant ship of the 2nd Century AD was about 55m long, 14m wide and 13m from deck to keel.

Mainsail
The ship was driven by a large square sail.

Artemon mast
Carried the small bow spritsail, which was used to help steering.

Swan's head
Ships often had a carved swan's head, representing the Egyptian goddess Isis, protector of sailors.

Steering oars
There were two, each with its own tiller.

Cargo hold
Cargo included wine, oil, grain and cloth.

RICH TRADERS

Successful merchants and bankers were the richest men in the Roman empire. Many of them made fortunes from shipping the vital cargoes on which the empire depended. They lived in great luxury and held enormous power, for even emperors needed to borrow their money. Some rich merchants succeeded in becoming the Emperor of Rome by using their wealth to buy the support of imperial soldiers.

Tiller

Poopdeck

Poopdeck shelter

ANIMAL TRANSPORT

Wild animals such as panthers and lions were shipped to major cities from Africa and the Middle East. They were taken to Roman amphitheatres, to be used in fighting contests. The caged animals were handled at the docks by slave workers.

Viking longship

FIGUREHEAD

Some longships had an elaborately carved animal on the forepost – the pointed structure built up from the ship's bow. This figurehead, originally covered in gold leaf, is from a beautifully decorated funeral ship found in Norway.

ATLANTIC EXPLORATION

Longships carried Viking explorers across the North Atlantic Ocean to the Faroes, Iceland, Greenland and to North America, which the Vikings called "Vinland". The orange shading on the map above shows the Viking empire.

WEATHER VANE

Made of gilded bronze, this intricate weather vane is a superb example of Viking art. It once flew at the head of a longship's mast. Weather vanes were used to show the steersman the direction of the wind.

After the fall of the Roman empire, the Viking longship emerged as the most important vessel of the open seas. First recorded in the late 700s, the longship was built in Denmark, Norway and Sweden. It carried Viking warriors to plunder every country in western Europe and Russia, as well as North America.

Like the ancient Egyptians, the Vikings sometimes buried ships at warriors' funerals, and several have been found and studied. A famous longship found at Gokstad, in Norway, is 23 metres long. Like all Viking ships, it was clinker-built, which means that its hull was made from overlapping planks. It sailed well and, by lowering its single mast and sail, could also be rowed. It was narrow and sat shallow in the water, which meant that it could be rowed up rivers with ease. The Gokstad longship was rowed by 16 rowers each side. The Vikings used their sea-chests as rowing benches. Many longships were much bigger than the Gokstad; the *Ormen Lange*, or "Long Serpent", owned by King Olaf Tryggvason of Norway (995-1000), had 34 oars each side.

WARRIOR

A Viking warrior's main weapons were a battle-axe and a long sword. Wealthier warriors wore a helmet and a shirt of linked iron rings.

Steersman

Steering oar

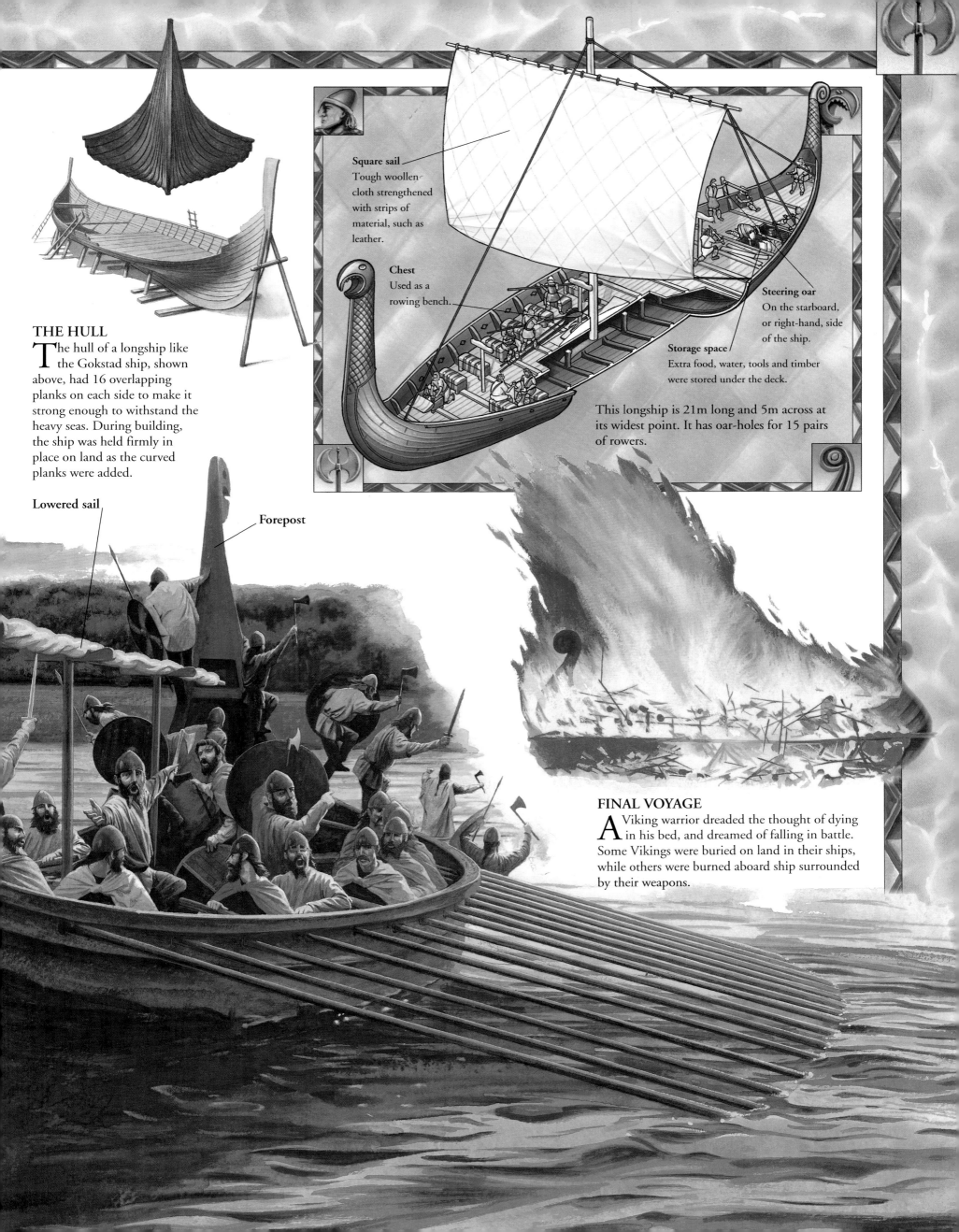

THE HULL

The hull of a longship like the Gokstad ship, shown above, had 16 overlapping planks on each side to make it strong enough to withstand the heavy seas. During building, the ship was held firmly in place on land as the curved planks were added.

Lowered sail

Forepost

Square sail
Tough woollen cloth strengthened with strips of material, such as leather.

Chest
Used as a rowing bench.

Steering oar
On the starboard, or right-hand, side of the ship.

Storage space
Extra food, water, tools and timber were stored under the deck.

This longship is 21m long and 5m across at its widest point. It has oar-holes for 15 pairs of rowers.

FINAL VOYAGE

A Viking warrior dreaded the thought of dying in his bed, and dreamed of falling in battle. Some Vikings were buried on land in their ships, while others were burned aboard ship surrounded by their weapons.

Hansa trading cog

"The French put their ships in readiness, like the skilled seamen and good fighters they were, and set the cog Christopher, *which they had taken from the English that same year, in the van with a big company of Genoese crossbowmen on board to defend it and harass the English."*

Jean Froissart *Chronicles*, 1340

A new kind of ship began to appear in Europe from about 1250. Called a cog, it still had many features used by earlier shipbuilders. Just like a Viking longship, the cog had a clinker-built hull, a single mast and a square sail. But there were important differences. The cog had a straight keel, a cargo hold below deck and a hinged rudder for steering.

These ships were used by the great cities of northern Germany that made up the trading and commercial alliance known as the Hanseatic League. Because of this, they are often called Hansa cogs. They carried Europe's cargoes until the early fifteenth century. They also served as useful troop carriers in times of war, when their two "castles" acted as firing platforms for archers and crossbowmen.

SEA CASTLES

In 1340 English longbow archers helped to win the Battle of Sluys, a famous sea battle against the French fleet. They fired their dreaded "arrow storm" from the bow and stern castles of troop-filled cogs.

STEERING BY RUDDER

A cog's helmsman steered the ship by moving the tiller – a bar fixed to the top of the rudder. This was a far more efficient way to steer a ship than the steering oar, and was an important advance in ship design.

Rudder

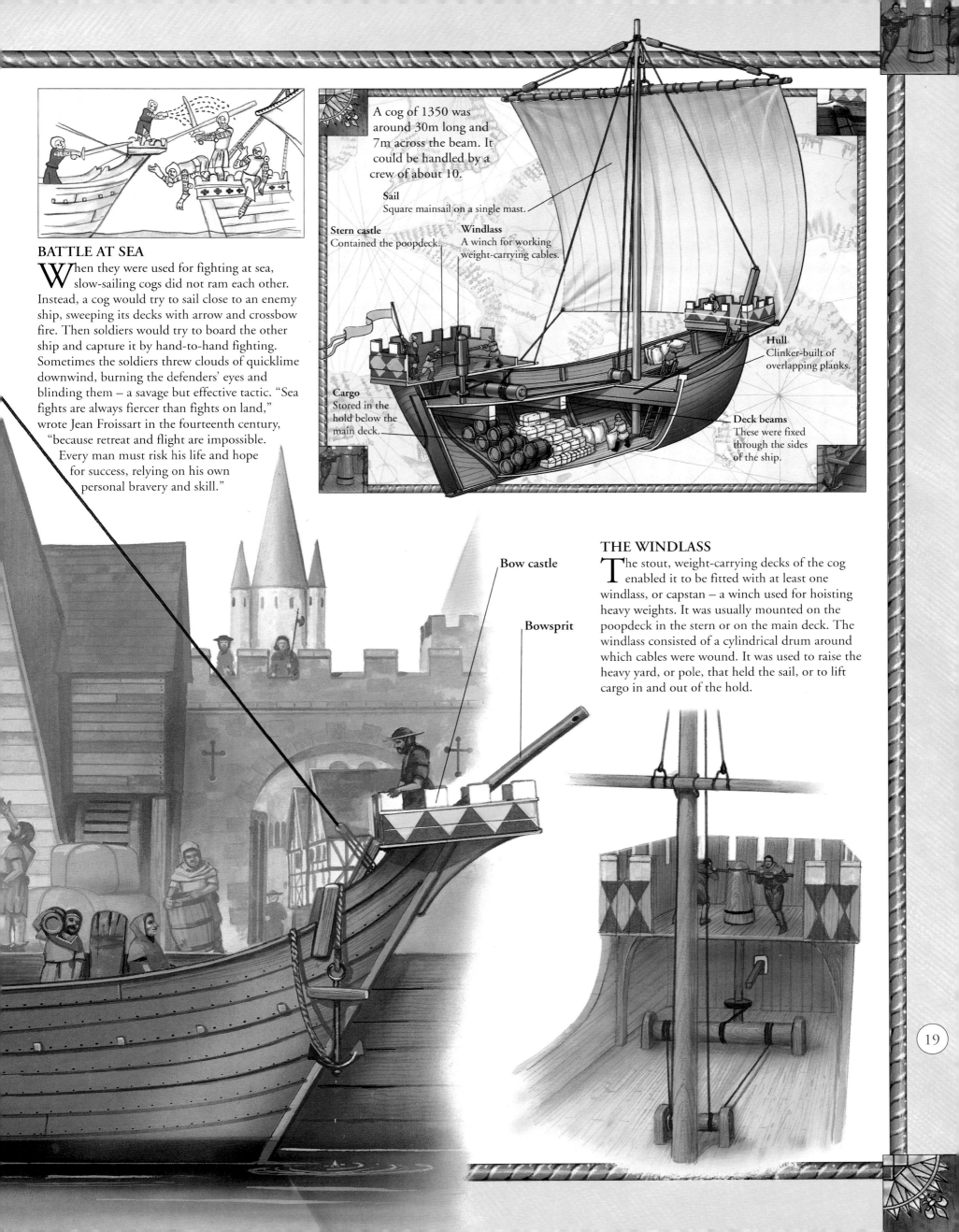

BATTLE AT SEA

When they were used for fighting at sea, slow-sailing cogs did not ram each other. Instead, a cog would try to sail close to an enemy ship, sweeping its decks with arrow and crossbow fire. Then soldiers would try to board the other ship and capture it by hand-to-hand fighting. Sometimes the soldiers threw clouds of quicklime downwind, burning the defenders' eyes and blinding them – a savage but effective tactic. "Sea fights are always fiercer than fights on land," wrote Jean Froissart in the fourteenth century, "because retreat and flight are impossible. Every man must risk his life and hope for success, relying on his own personal bravery and skill."

A cog of 1350 was around 30m long and 7m across the beam. It could be handled by a crew of about 10.

Sail
Square mainsail on a single mast.

Stern castle
Contained the poopdeck.

Windlass
A winch for working weight-carrying cables.

Hull
Clinker-built of overlapping planks.

Cargo
Stored in the hold below the main deck.

Deck beams
These were fixed through the sides of the ship.

Bow castle

Bowsprit

THE WINDLASS

The stout, weight-carrying decks of the cog enabled it to be fitted with at least one windlass, or capstan – a winch used for hoisting heavy weights. It was usually mounted on the poopdeck in the stern or on the main deck. The windlass consisted of a cylindrical drum around which cables were wound. It was used to raise the heavy yard, or pole, that held the sail, or to lift cargo in and out of the hold.

Caravel explorer

COAT OF ARMS

In 1493, Columbus was granted his own coat of arms by King Ferdinand and Queen Isabella of Spain.

In the late 1400s European shipbuilders changed the design of the hull from the clinker-built style to the more streamlined caravel style. This meant laying the outer planks edge to edge over a strong framework built up from the keel. Using this method, Portuguese and Spanish caravels emerged as ships capable of making record-breaking voyages of discovery. The caravel opened sea routes to the Americas and the Far East. The *Niña*, illustrated below, was the favourite ship of Christopher Columbus, sailing on three of his four voyages to the New World. The caravel was a small ship, with a rounded bow and a square stern. It was the first European ship to carry the full "ship rig" of foremast, mainmast and mizzenmast. Bigger caravels had a fourth mast at the stern, called a "countermizzen".

PUNISHMENT AT SEA

A sailor who swore or answered back to officers was tied to the mast and gagged with a wooden bar, called a belaying pin, until his mouth bled.

NAVIGATION

The astrolabe, above, measured the height and position of the Sun and stars. From this, the ship's position could be calculated. The traverse board, on the right, recorded the ship's course.

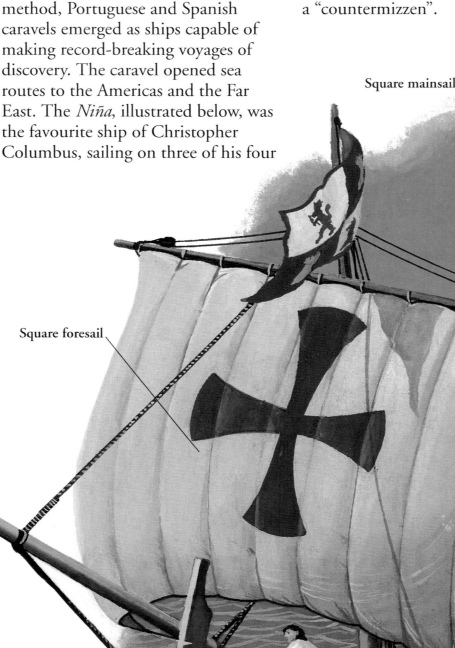

Square mainsail

Square foresail

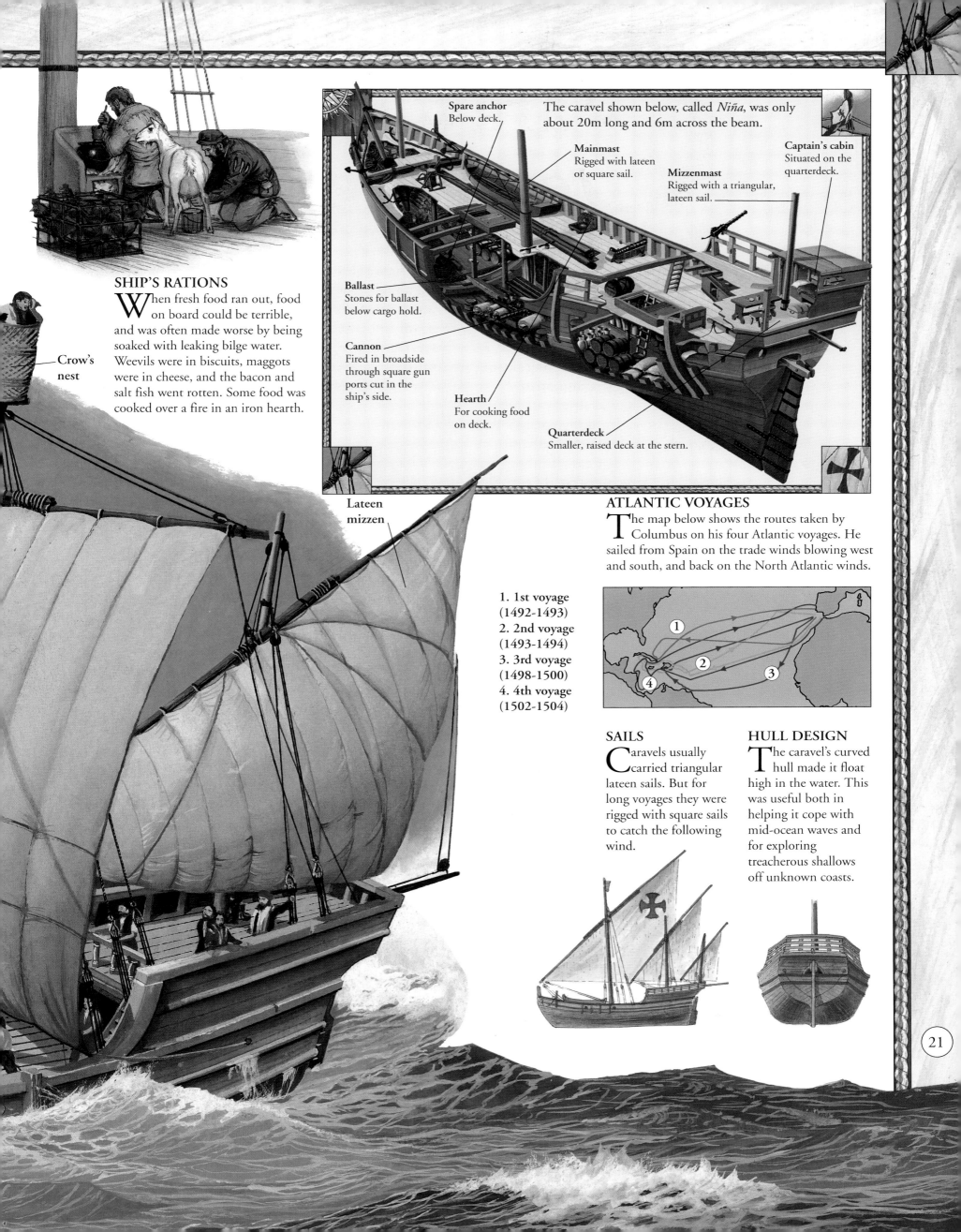

SHIP'S RATIONS

When fresh food ran out, food on board could be terrible, and was often made worse by being soaked with leaking bilge water. Weevils were in biscuits, maggots were in cheese, and the bacon and salt fish went rotten. Some food was cooked over a fire in an iron hearth.

Crow's nest

Lateen mizzen

The caravel shown below, called *Niña*, was only about 20m long and 6m across the beam.

Spare anchor
Below deck.

Mainmast
Rigged with lateen or square sail.

Mizzenmast
Rigged with a triangular, lateen sail.

Captain's cabin
Situated on the quarterdeck.

Ballast
Stones for ballast below cargo hold.

Cannon
Fired in broadside through square gun ports cut in the ship's side.

Hearth
For cooking food on deck.

Quarterdeck
Smaller, raised deck at the stern.

ATLANTIC VOYAGES

The map below shows the routes taken by Columbus on his four Atlantic voyages. He sailed from Spain on the trade winds blowing west and south, and back on the North Atlantic winds.

1. 1st voyage (1492-1493)
2. 2nd voyage (1493-1494)
3. 3rd voyage (1498-1500)
4. 4th voyage (1502-1504)

SAILS

Caravels usually carried triangular lateen sails. But for long voyages they were rigged with square sails to catch the following wind.

HULL DESIGN

The caravel's curved hull made it float high in the water. This was useful both in helping it cope with mid-ocean waves and for exploring treacherous shallows off unknown coasts.

17th-century

Warship

"Our condition is like to be very miserable. Our ships are extreme foul, winter drawing on, our victuals expiring, all stores failing, and our men falling sick through badness of drink and through eating their victuals boiled in salt water for two months' space."

Admiral Robert Blake to Oliver Cromwell, August 1655

FLAGS

Flags showed which country the ship belonged to and who commanded it. By the 1650s, flags were used to pass messages to other ships in the same fleet.

Between about 1570 and 1620, the galleon became the world's most powerful type of warship. It was armed with batteries of guns mounted to fire broadside, through ports cut in the ship's sides. Over the next 50 years the galleon developed into the two- or three-decked battleship of 100 guns or more, displacing over 2,000 tonnes and crewed by 800 or more sailors or troops. These great and beautiful ships were works of art, blazing with gold leaf and paint – but, as the above quote written in 1655 shows, life on board was tough.

THE CREW

The captain was in overall control of the ship, but he often relied on the ship's master, a more experienced and trained sailor, who commanded the seamen. The ship also carried a fighting force of gunners and soldiers as well as craftsmen. The ship's boy was responsible for keeping the ship clean.

1. The captain
2. The ship's master
3. A seaman
4. The ship's boy

DECK FIGHTERS

As the ship approached an enemy vessel, lightweight swivel guns mounted on the rails sprayed its decks with lethal grape-shot. Some early warships carried a company of archers. Although they mainly fought on land, they could also defend their ship at sea if necessary.

Spritsail

Bowsprit

Beakhead

Anchor

Prow

Main yardarm
A horizontal spar from which the largest sail on the main mast hung.

AT THE MASTHEAD

Where the sections of the masts joined, round platforms called "tops" helped the sailors work aloft. They also served as look-out posts and carried sharp-shooters.

Forecastle
A raised section at the ship's bow housing the crew's living quarters.

Whipstaff
A vertical lever connected to the rudder for steering the ship.

Gun ports
Holes cut in the hull for guns to fire through.

Galley
Area where food was prepared, generally by boiling.

A 17th-century warship was about 40m long, with a keel 30m long, and a beam (width) of 11m. It carried a crew of about 300 sailors and 100 soldiers, and was armed with about 40 guns.

Fore topsail

Main topsail

BEAUTY AND FIRE-POWER

A big royal flagship like *Kronan* was built to show the wealth and power of the king or state. It carried rich carvings outside, even around the gun ports. The English *Sovereign of the Seas*, launched in 1637, wore so much gold leaf that its enemies called it "Golden Devil". But if properly looked after they served for many more years than modern warships.

AT THE HELM

A galleon was steered by means of a lever called the whipstaff operated by the ship's helmsman. As the whipstaff was below deck, the helmsman could not see where the ship was going. He had to follow instructions shouted down through a hatch to him by an officer on deck. When the captain ordered a change of course, the helmsman pushed the whipstaff to one side, which swung the ship's rudder round and turned the ship.

Forecourse

Mainshroud

SERVING THE GUNS

The ship's value in battle depended on how fast the guns could be reloaded and fired. After each shot the gun had to be sponged clean of fragments that were still burning, reloaded with a rammed-in powder charge and shot, then run out again. Ten or more men were needed to crew each of the heaviest guns.

Steamship

"It can seem that the steady progress of iron and steam was one of unfettered progress. The Great Eastern stands as a reminder that there is always a price to be paid."
Anthony Burton *The Rise and Fall of British Shipbuilding*

By the 1830s, sailing ships were being fitted with steam engines for extra power on ocean voyages, but the amount of coal they could carry was small. After his steamships the *Great Western* and the *Great Britain*, launched in 1837 and 1843, the British engineer Isambard Kingdom Brunel planned an even bigger iron ship. This was the *Great Eastern*, shown below, which was built to carry enough coal to steam to India and Australia and was launched in 1858.

Driven by sail, paddlewheels and a stern propeller, this giant steamship was designed to carry 4,000 passengers and 6,000 tonnes of cargo. It was the biggest ship built before the 1890s, but it was dogged by problems and was a failure as a passenger ship. The *Great Eastern* laid the first successful Atlantic telegraph cable in 1866, but was scrapped in 1888.

GIANT PADDLES

The *Great Eastern*'s two huge paddlewheels were each 17 metres in diameter. They added almost 11 metres to the overall width of the ship and had an effect similar to giant brakes, which ruined its abilities as a sailing ship.

PUSH-PULL ENGINES

Each of the *Great Eastern*'s giant paddlewheels was driven by a huge two-cylinder engine. The oscillating engines pushed and pulled the paddlewheel crankshafts around in great circles. With an enormous piston and piston-rod, each cylinder weighed nearly 30 tonnes. These massive engines, with their unguarded, whirling cranks and couplings, were at once cumbersome, dangerous and deafening.

Starboard paddlewheel

Lifeboat

PROPELLER

The massive four-bladed screw propeller at the stern was over seven metres across and weighed over 36 tonnes. It was driven from a separate engine room by a row of four cylinders, each of which, if required, could work independently of the others.

Iron tube mast

Cable-winding gear
The cable was copper wire covered with tar, jute, and gutta percha.

Paddle engine room
Four boilers powered the 1,000hp engine.

Mast
Six masts held 5,336 sq m of sail.

Screw engine room
Six boilers powered the 1,600hp engine.

Cable-laying storage tank
Each was deep enough for a man to stand up in.

Watertight doors
For controlling flooding.

Coal bunkers
To fuel the screw and paddle engines.

The *Great Eastern* was driven by sails, paddlewheels and a propeller. It was 211m long and weighed 27,838 tonnes. Its grand passenger accommodation was taken out when it was used for laying the transatlantic cable.

Sails furled to yards

Wire rigging

LAYING CABLE

The *Great Eastern* was the only ship in the world big enough to carry enough cable (4,022 kilometres, weighing 4,673 tonnes) to stretch across the Atlantic seabed from Ireland to Newfoundland. The task was achieved in July 1866.

Ironclad

"Our hope, our one chance, is the Monitor.*"*
Gideon Welles,
US Navy Secretary, 1862

STEEL SHOT

Steel shot were needed to pierce armour plate. The *Merrimack* went into battle before hers were ready, and so she fired explosive shells instead. The *Monitor*'s shot were fired with reduced powder charges, and most bounced off the *Merrimack*'s sloping armour.

By the late 1830s, wooden sailing ships faced a new threat – rifled cannon firing explosive shells instead of solid shot. Wooden ships simply could not withstand this shellfire. Metal armour was needed, and so by 1860 the French and British navies had built warships protected by iron plates – "ironclads". The first was France's *Gloire,* a wooden steam frigate with an iron "belt" above the waterline, followed by Britain's all-iron *Warrior*. During the American Civil War

(1861-65), steam-powered ironclads met in battle for the first time. The South built the *Merrimack*, and the North replied by building the *Monitor*, shown below, with a rotating armoured turret. Conditions inside the ships would have been extremely hot. They fought in 1862 in Virginia, blasting each other at close range for over two hours. Neither was able to pierce the armour of the other and the battle ended in stalemate. A new age in naval warfare had begun.

LAUNCH

The *Monitor* took only four months to build, and was ready for launch in January 1862. Many experts doubted that she would even float. To prove them wrong, the ship's designer, John Ericsson, stood on deck during the *Monitor*'s successful launch in New York.

(1)

(2)

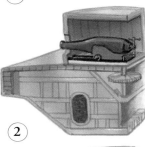

(3)

IRONCLAD HULLS

The *Warrior* (1861) had a hull with an armoured belt lined on the inside with teak wood (1). The *Monitor* (1862) had a flat hull which lay low in the water to give little for enemy ships to fire at (2). The *Buffel* (1868) had a stronger hull with a rounded bottom to enable it to cope with the seas (3).

Smoke stack

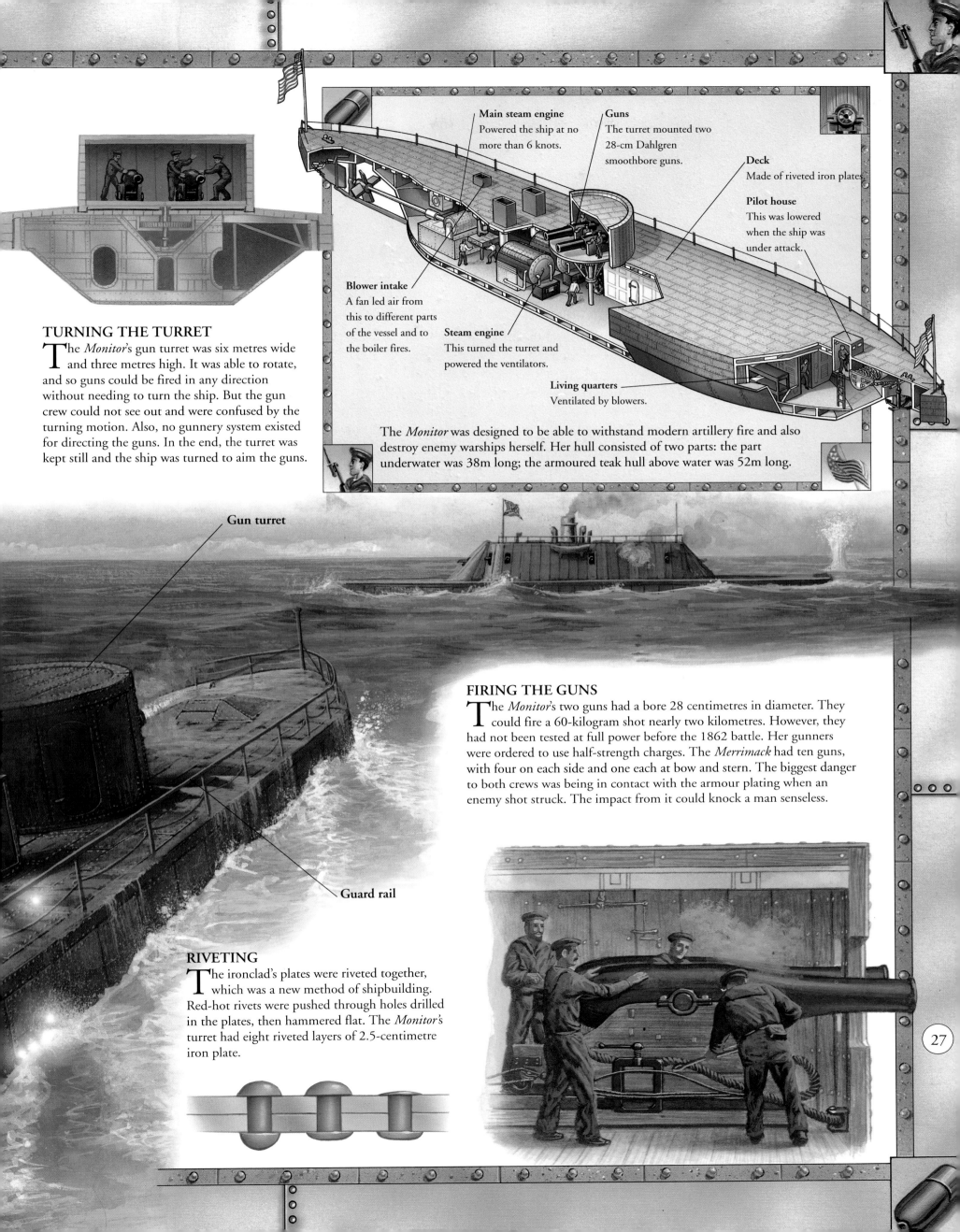

Main steam engine	Guns
Powered the ship at no more than 6 knots.	The turret mounted two 28-cm Dahlgren smoothbore guns.

Deck
Made of riveted iron plates.

Pilot house
This was lowered when the ship was under attack.

Blower intake
A fan led air from this to different parts of the vessel and to the boiler fires.

Steam engine
This turned the turret and powered the ventilators.

Living quarters
Ventilated by blowers.

The *Monitor* was designed to be able to withstand modern artillery fire and also destroy enemy warships herself. Her hull consisted of two parts: the part underwater was 38m long; the armoured teak hull above water was 52m long.

TURNING THE TURRET

The *Monitor*'s gun turret was six metres wide and three metres high. It was able to rotate, and so guns could be fired in any direction without needing to turn the ship. But the gun crew could not see out and were confused by the turning motion. Also, no gunnery system existed for directing the guns. In the end, the turret was kept still and the ship was turned to aim the guns.

Gun turret

Guard rail

FIRING THE GUNS

The *Monitor*'s two guns had a bore 28 centimetres in diameter. They could fire a 60-kilogram shot nearly two kilometres. However, they had not been tested at full power before the 1862 battle. Her gunners were ordered to use half-strength charges. The *Merrimack* had ten guns, with four on each side and one each at bow and stern. The biggest danger to both crews was being in contact with the armour plating when an enemy shot struck. The impact from it could knock a man senseless.

RIVETING

The ironclad's plates were riveted together, which was a new method of shipbuilding. Red-hot rivets were pushed through holes drilled in the plates, then hammered flat. The *Monitor*'s turret had eight riveted layers of 2.5-centimetre iron plate.

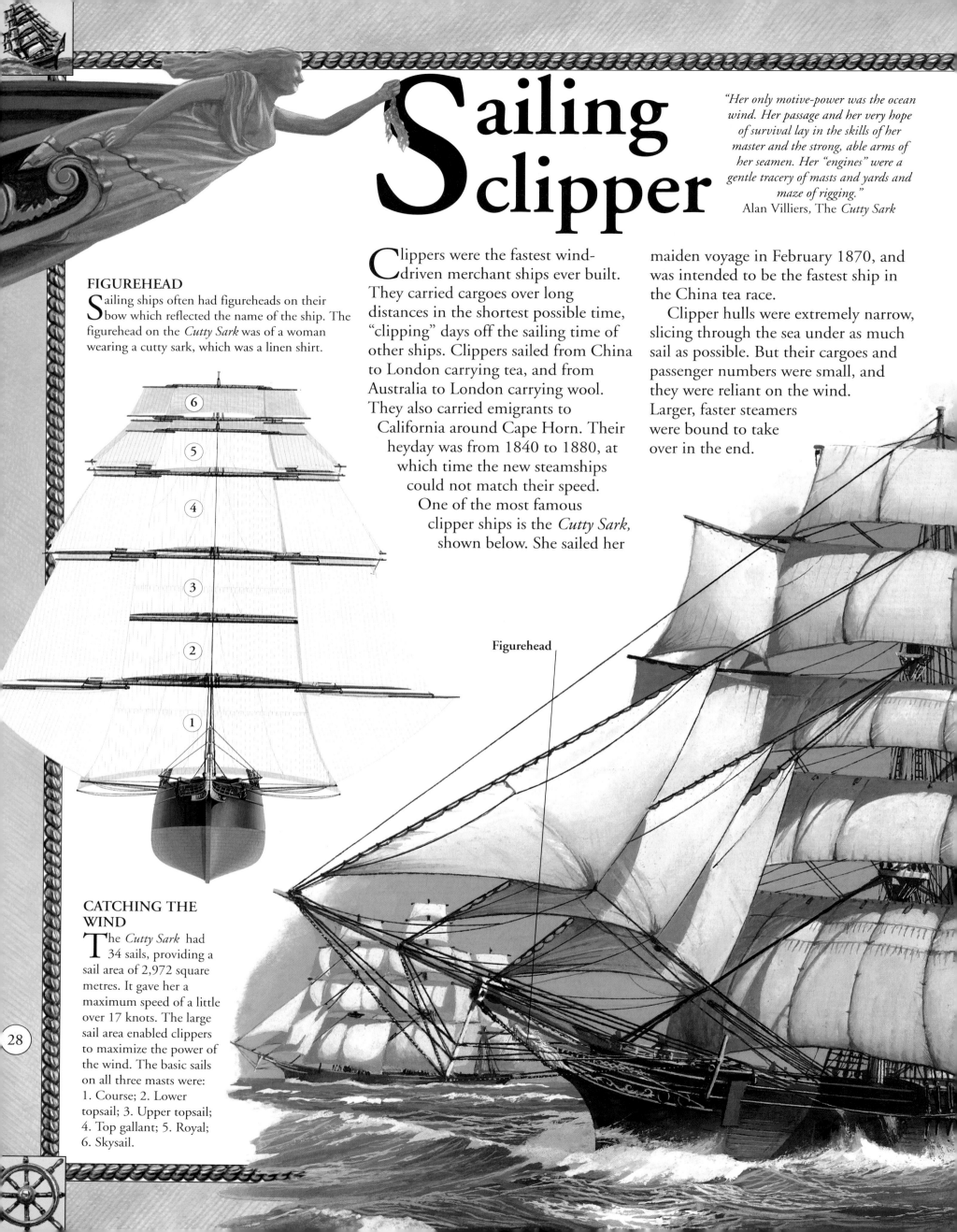

Sailing clipper

"Her only motive-power was the ocean wind. Her passage and her very hope of survival lay in the skills of her master and the strong, able arms of her seamen. Her "engines" were a gentle tracery of masts and yards and maze of rigging."
Alan Villiers, The *Cutty Sark*

FIGUREHEAD

Sailing ships often had figureheads on their bow which reflected the name of the ship. The figurehead on the *Cutty Sark* was of a woman wearing a cutty sark, which was a linen shirt.

Clippers were the fastest wind-driven merchant ships ever built. They carried cargoes over long distances in the shortest possible time, "clipping" days off the sailing time of other ships. Clippers sailed from China to London carrying tea, and from Australia to London carrying wool. They also carried emigrants to California around Cape Horn. Their heyday was from 1840 to 1880, at which time the new steamships could not match their speed. One of the most famous clipper ships is the *Cutty Sark*, shown below. She sailed her

maiden voyage in February 1870, and was intended to be the fastest ship in the China tea race.

Clipper hulls were extremely narrow, slicing through the sea under as much sail as possible. But their cargoes and passenger numbers were small, and they were reliant on the wind. Larger, faster steamers were bound to take over in the end.

Figurehead

CATCHING THE WIND

The *Cutty Sark* had 34 sails, providing a sail area of 2,972 square metres. It gave her a maximum speed of a little over 17 knots. The large sail area enabled clippers to maximize the power of the wind. The basic sails on all three masts were:
1. Course; 2. Lower topsail; 3. Upper topsail; 4. Top gallant; 5. Royal; 6. Skysail.

WOOL TRADE

Clippers used the winds known as the "Roaring Forties" to sail to Australia via the Cape of Good Hope, just below southern Africa, returning eastwards around Cape Horn, which is just below southern America.

Staysail
Helped the ship sail at an angle to the wind.

Counterstern
Helped protect this part of the ship from waves.

Hull
Sheathed in copper plating below the waterline to prevent barnacles growing, which would slow the ship down.

Stunsails
These small extra sails could be added to all three masts.

Jib
Also helped ship sail at angle to wind.

Cargo hold
Carried only small cargoes because of the narrow hull.

The Clipper was designed to sail as fast as possible. Its overall length was 86m, and it had a height of 64.8m.

MANNING THE YARDS

Footropes helped bare-footed sailors man the yards, or poles, to which the sails were attached, so that they could set and shorten sail. It could be a hazardous job, especially in cold or rough weather. Footropes sometimes broke, and accidents were common.

Spanker

AT THE HELM

A clipper's wheel was in the open, on the poopdeck. In stormy weather, steering was an exhausting job. The helmsman had to watch out for every shift in the wind, to prevent damage to the sails.

World War 1 battleship

"As the German ships one after another emerged from the mist, all the British battleships whose range was clear opened a terrific fire upon them. The German van, the formidable Königs, *saw the whole horizon as far as the eye could reach alive with flashes. The concussion of the shell storm broke upon the German vessels."*
Winston Churchill *The World Crisis*

By the 1880s, improvements in steam engines meant that warships no longer needed masts and sails. Battleships were large, heavily armoured steamships with powerful, long-range guns. These were breech-loading guns, which meant that shells were loaded into the breech behind the barrel. This allowed gun crews to load and fire from inside an armoured turret.

By 1900 the biggest danger to the new battleships was powered torpedoes, fired from fast boats. Then, in 1906, came Britain's *Dreadnought* battleship, which carried ten heavy guns and could steam faster than any other battleship afloat. Other navies began to build similar ships, and at the beginning of World War 1, Britain had 20 "Dreadnoughts" to Germany's 14. The two battleship fleets fought only once, at the Battle of Jutland in 1916, and the result was indecisive. The British fleet lost more men and a heavier tonnage of ships, while the smaller German fleet fled to base and never risked another battle.

FLAG SIGNALS

In World War 1, flags were still hoisted to act as signals. Flag signals were used to communicate between battleships and to direct fleet movements. Each flag stood for a letter or a code word.

LOADING THE GUNS

Shells and cordite charges were hoisted to gun turrets from the ammunition magazine below the waterline. Two men loaded the gun, while two more held the next shell and charge ready. All loaders wore long gloves and hoods to protect their skin from the scorching flash when the gun was fired. *Dreadnought* could fire an eight-gun salvo. This meant that eight of its 10 big guns could fire in the same direction at the same time.

MUSKETRY DRILL

Sailors still had to practise firing a rifle, and so there was regular musketry drill. The long range of the battleships' big guns made it impossible for ships to get close enough to each other to use rifles, but sailors had to be ready to fight on shore if necessary.

Boom for anti-torpedo net

Radio aerial

Light 54-kg gun

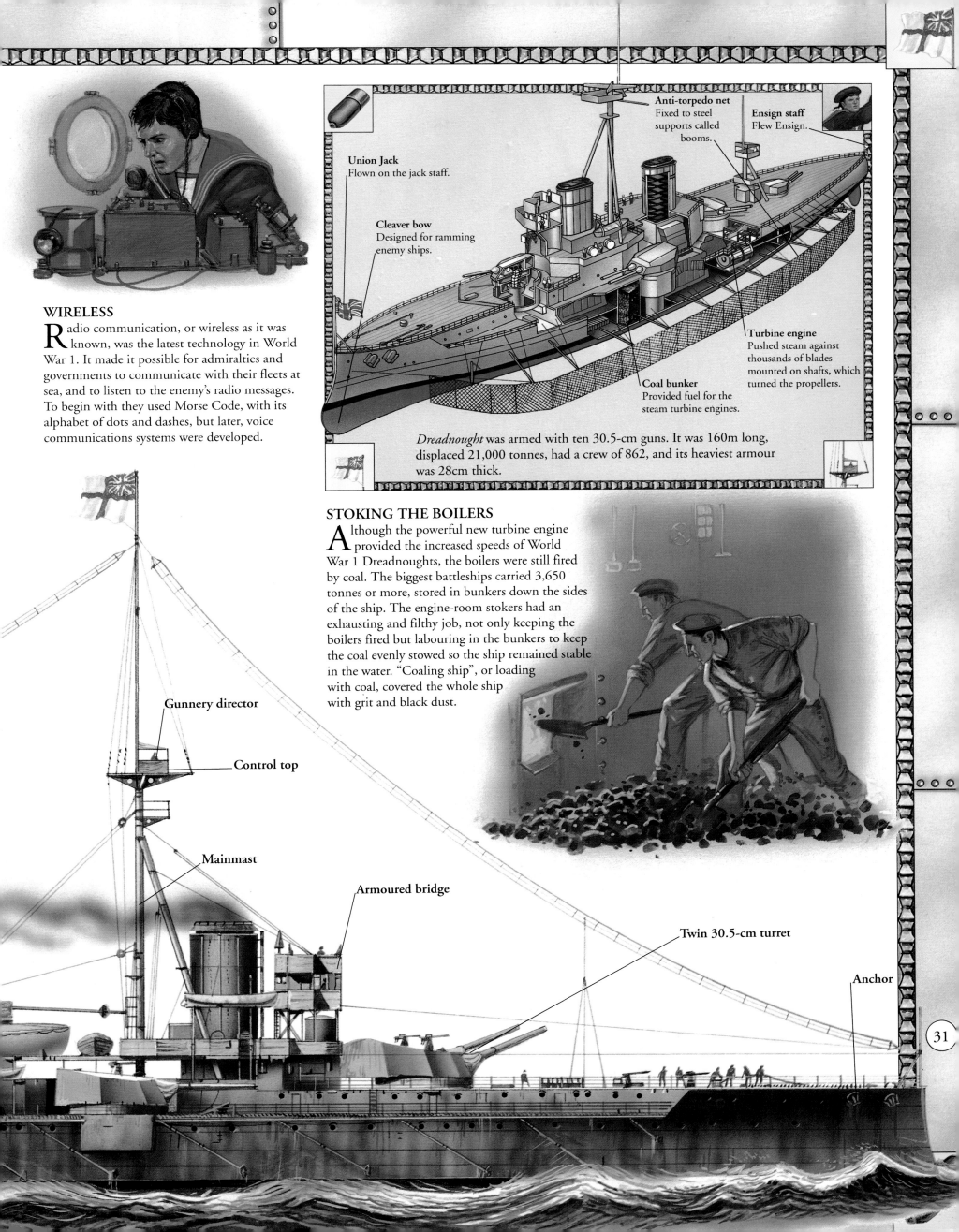

WIRELESS

Radio communication, or wireless as it was known, was the latest technology in World War 1. It made it possible for admiralties and governments to communicate with their fleets at sea, and to listen to the enemy's radio messages. To begin with they used Morse Code, with its alphabet of dots and dashes, but later, voice communications systems were developed.

Anti-torpedo net
Fixed to steel supports called booms.

Ensign staff
Flew Ensign.

Union Jack
Flown on the jack staff.

Cleaver bow
Designed for ramming enemy ships.

Turbine engine
Pushed steam against thousands of blades mounted on shafts, which turned the propellers.

Coal bunker
Provided fuel for the steam turbine engines.

Dreadnought was armed with ten 30.5-cm guns. It was 160m long, displaced 21,000 tonnes, had a crew of 862, and its heaviest armour was 28cm thick.

STOKING THE BOILERS

Although the powerful new turbine engine provided the increased speeds of World War 1 Dreadnoughts, the boilers were still fired by coal. The biggest battleships carried 3,650 tonnes or more, stored in bunkers down the sides of the ship. The engine-room stokers had an exhausting and filthy job, not only keeping the boilers fired but labouring in the bunkers to keep the coal evenly stowed so the ship remained stable in the water. "Coaling ship", or loading with coal, covered the whole ship with grit and black dust.

Gunnery director

Control top

Mainmast

Armoured bridge

Twin 30.5-cm turret

Anchor

Luxury 1930s liner

SHIP-TO-SHORE STREAMERS

The gaiety and excitement of departure was helped by the passengers' custom of throwing paper streamers from the ship to the dock, as symbols of breaking ties with the land.

STORES FOR A SINGLE CROSSING

The range of food, drink, and stores shipped by *Queen Mary* for a single Atlantic crossing – enough for 1,432 first class, 1,510 second class, and 1,058 third class passengers – is shown below, together with some of the fixed items used in the building of the ship.

From the 1880s until the coming of cheap air travel in the 1960s, the quickest and most comfortable way of crossing the Atlantic was by passenger liner. The big liners of Europe and America competed for the "Blue Riband of the Atlantic", awarded for the quickest crossing. The luxury, comfort and service provided for first class passengers was the best in the world. Even for the poorest passengers in the third class or steerage, seeking a new life in America, their liner cabins were usually the finest housing they had ever known. In the 1930s, France's *Normandie* and Britain's *Queen Mary* were the biggest, fastest ships of that time.

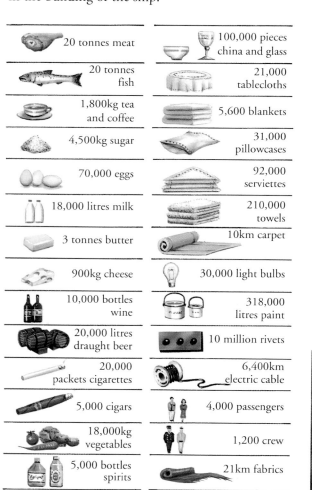

20 tonnes meat	100,000 pieces china and glass
20 tonnes fish	21,000 tablecloths
1,800kg tea and coffee	5,600 blankets
4,500kg sugar	31,000 pillowcases
70,000 eggs	92,000 serviettes
18,000 litres milk	210,000 towels
3 tonnes butter	10km carpet
900kg cheese	30,000 light bulbs
10,000 bottles wine	318,000 litres paint
20,000 litres draught beer	10 million rivets
20,000 packets cigarettes	6,400km electric cable
5,000 cigars	4,000 passengers
18,000kg vegetables	1,200 crew
5,000 bottles spirits	21km fabrics

Crow's nest

Fore funnel

Bridge

Midship's funnel

Aft funnel

Lifeboats

QUEEN MARY

FROM KEEL TO FUNNEL

From keel to funnel-tops, *Queen Mary* would have towered 10 metres higher than the Statue of Liberty's upraised torch, if the two giant structures could have been placed side by side.

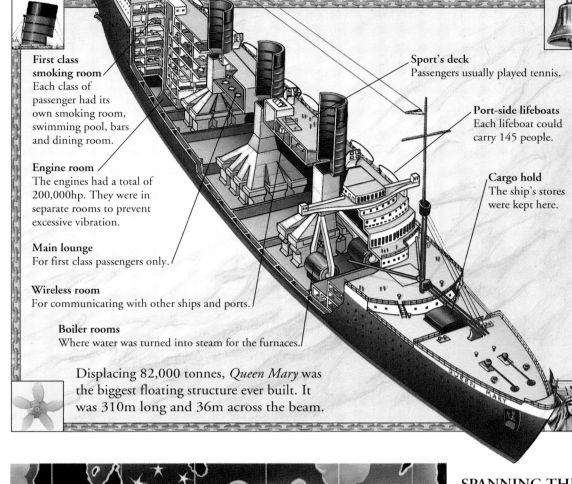

First class smoking room
Each class of passenger had its own smoking room, swimming pool, bars and dining room.

Engine room
The engines had a total of 200,000hp. They were in separate rooms to prevent excessive vibration.

Main lounge
For first class passengers only.

Wireless room
For communicating with other ships and ports.

Boiler rooms
Where water was turned into steam for the furnaces.

Sport's deck
Passengers usually played tennis.

Port-side lifeboats
Each lifeboat could carry 145 people.

Cargo hold
The ship's stores were kept here.

Displacing 82,000 tonnes, *Queen Mary* was the biggest floating structure ever built. It was 310m long and 36m across the beam.

SPANNING THE ATLANTIC

This enormous map and clock were displayed on the wall of *Queen Mary*'s main dining hall. With New York and London on opposite sides of the North Atlantic, it featured a moving model which showed the ship's position throughout the voyage.

SOCIAL LIFE

A seat at the captain's table was regarded as an honour by the richest and most famous passengers. They were also entertained with dances, parties, and sporting activities. With the exception of France's *Normandie*, which it was built to match, *Queen Mary* offered passengers more luxurious features than any liner that has ever been built.

World War 2 submarine

"The key to German power at sea lies below the surface. Give us submarines and we shall have the teeth to attack."
Grand-Admiral Raeder to Adolf Hitler, 1934

In World War 1, submarines had shown themselves to be a deadly new type of underwater warship. By the start of World War 2 (1939-1945), the world's leading navies had all built submarine fleets. Germany had its U-boats. The German *U-Boot* is short for *Unterseeboot*, meaning literally "undersea boat". U-boats came close to winning the Battle of the Atlantic between 1940 and 1943, when they sank thousands of tonnes of allied shipping thus preventing vital supplies reaching Britain.

The Type VII U-boat played a leading role in the Atlantic battle. It was powered by diesel engines on the surface and by an electric motor when submerged. The U-boat shown below carried 14 torpedoes, fired from four tubes in the bow and one in the stern. There was also an 8.8-centimetre gun on the deck for surface fighting.

UP PERISCOPE!

The periscope was raised to give the captain an all-round view from under water. Red lighting in the submarine helped him to see more clearly through the periscope.

Mooring cleat

DIVING AND SURFACING

Submarines dive by flooding the ballast tanks that surround the inner hull where the crew live and work. To surface again, the seawater is forced back out of the ballast tanks by compressed air.

1. Submarine on the surface: top vents are shut, and outer ballast tanks full of air, giving the submarine buoyancy.

2. Submarine diving: top vents and bottom vents are open, seawater is flooding into outer ballast tanks and driving air out through vents.

3. Submarine surfacing: top vents are shut again, and compressed air is forcing seawater out of outer ballast tanks.

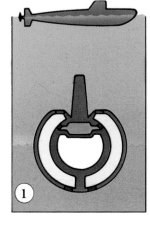

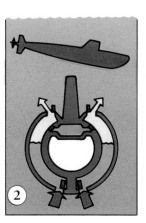

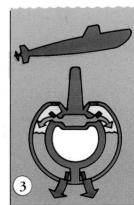

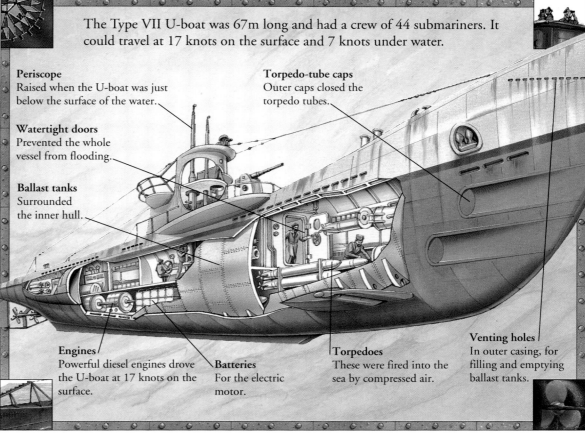

The Type VII U-boat was 67m long and had a crew of 44 submariners. It could travel at 17 knots on the surface and 7 knots under water.

Periscope
Raised when the U-boat was just below the surface of the water.

Torpedo-tube caps
Outer caps closed the torpedo tubes.

Watertight doors
Prevented the whole vessel from flooding.

Ballast tanks
Surrounded the inner hull.

Engines
Powerful diesel engines drove the U-boat at 17 knots on the surface.

Batteries
For the electric motor.

Torpedoes
These were fired into the sea by compressed air.

Venting holes
In outer casing, for filling and emptying ballast tanks.

LIFE ON BOARD

There was little room on a U-boat. Folding bunks behind the bow tubes could only be used when the spare torpedoes had been fired and the submarine was heading back to port. With no water for washing, submariners tended to suffer from boils and other skin complaints. It was also damp, which often made food turn mouldy.

8.8-cm deck gun

Conning tower

HUNTING SUBMARINES

Sonar – from "SOund NAvigation and Ranging" – was used by surface ships to detect submarines. A sound pulse or "ping" hit an object, and sent back an echo. The submarine crew heard the "ping" as a metallic tapping. The enemy ship dropped depth charges which exploded under water, forcing the submarine to surface and surrender, or blowing it apart.

PROPELLERS

Most submarines were driven by two propellers. Submarines carried a hydrophone that could detect the sounds of other propellers from surface ships or other submarines.

LOADING THE TUBES

Torpedo operators had an exhausting job when the time came to reload. The torpedo was lowered on to guide rails – a difficult and dangerous task if the submarine was rolling. Then it was hauled into the tube. The torpedo was launched into the sea with a blast of compressed air. As the torpedo shot forward, its own engine started up. This carried it to the target ship.

Aircraft carrier

Air search
radar scanner

Lifeboat

The first aircraft carriers were built at the end of World War 1 (1914-1918); too late to play an active part in that conflict. In World War 2 (1939-1945) they replaced the battleship as the most important heavy warship.

The air group (aircraft) on board a carrier includes fighters to shoot down enemy aircraft, and strike aircraft to attack enemy ships and land targets with bombs, torpedoes, and rockets. Modern carriers are the biggest and most complex warships ever built. The largest carriers are floating air bases, built to carry all the fuel, weapons and spares to keep their air groups flying and fighting. Nuclear-powered carriers can travel for almost two million kilometres without refuelling.

SHIP'S CREW

In addition to the captain, officers and seamen, half the crew are aviation personnel. A landing signals officer guides pilots down to a safe landing while fire crews stand by.
1. Captain
2. Landing Signals Officer (LSO)
3. Pilot
4. Fire crew
5. Officer

DEVELOPMENT OF THE CARRIER

Experiments with separate flying-off and landing-on decks proved too dangerous, so carriers were given single flight decks extending from bow to stern. The superstructure with the bridge and command centre were placed on the starboard side of the flight deck.

Landing Signals Officer control station

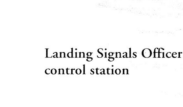

LIFE ON BOARD

The largest carriers are crewed by up to 6,000 men, who have to be fed three times a day, so a carrier's kitchens rarely close. The crew work hard but they also have to be entertained when they are off duty. Some carriers have shops, a cinema, satellite television and even their own television station on board broadcasting to the crew.

TAKE-OFF

By 1945, the dawn of the jet age, carrier planes were becoming so big and heavy that their engines could not launch them fast enough. They needed the extra punch of a catapult driven by steam from the ship's boilers. Each plane is hitched to it by a sling which falls away once the plane is airborne.

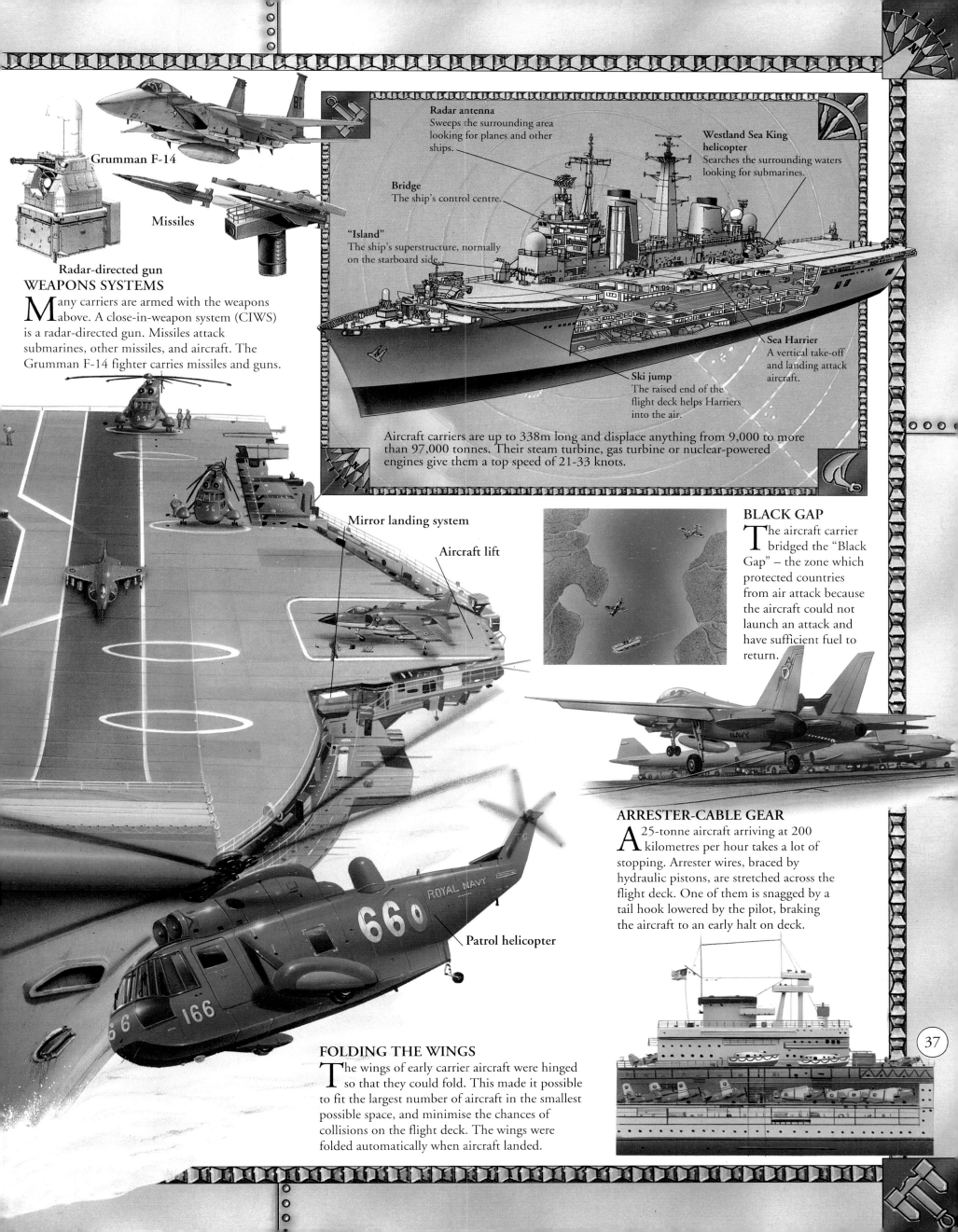

Grumman F-14

Missiles

Radar-directed gun

WEAPONS SYSTEMS

Many carriers are armed with the weapons above. A close-in-weapon system (CIWS) is a radar-directed gun. Missiles attack submarines, other missiles, and aircraft. The Grumman F-14 fighter carries missiles and guns.

Radar antenna
Sweeps the surrounding area looking for planes and other ships.

Westland Sea King helicopter
Searches the surrounding waters looking for submarines.

Bridge
The ship's control centre.

"Island"
The ship's superstructure, normally on the starboard side.

Sea Harrier
A vertical take-off and landing attack aircraft.

Ski jump
The raised end of the flight deck helps Harriers into the air.

Aircraft carriers are up to 338m long and displace anything from 9,000 to more than 97,000 tonnes. Their steam turbine, gas turbine or nuclear-powered engines give them a top speed of 21-33 knots.

Mirror landing system

Aircraft lift

BLACK GAP

The aircraft carrier bridged the "Black Gap" – the zone which protected countries from air attack because the aircraft could not launch an attack and have sufficient fuel to return.

ARRESTER-CABLE GEAR

A 25-tonne aircraft arriving at 200 kilometres per hour takes a lot of stopping. Arrester wires, braced by hydraulic pistons, are stretched across the flight deck. One of them is snagged by a tail hook lowered by the pilot, braking the aircraft to an early halt on deck.

ROYAL NAVY

66

166

Patrol helicopter

FOLDING THE WINGS

The wings of early carrier aircraft were hinged so that they could fold. This made it possible to fit the largest number of aircraft in the smallest possible space, and minimise the chances of collisions on the flight deck. The wings were folded automatically when aircraft landed.

Supertanker

"The most catastrophic spill out of the pipeline would be 60,000 barrels of oil. A 167,000-tonne tanker carries about one million barrels."
Charles Champion, Alaska pipeline coordinator, 1978

Crude oil, as pumped from the ground, is a vital energy source. Every developed country in the world depends on oil. It is used as fuel in power stations for generating electricity, and refined to make petrol and diesel fuels for all sorts of vehicles.

Since the 1960s, the world's demand for oil has produced the most gigantic ships ever built: supertankers. If a supertanker can carry over 200,000 tonnes of crude oil, people in the industry call it a VLCC, a "very large crude carrier". And if it is enormous enough to carry over 300,000 tonnes – that's equivalent to nearly two million barrels of oil – then they call it a ULCC, an "ultra-large crude carrier".

At 378 metres long and 50 metres wide, the supertanker *Globtik Tokyo* is certainly ultra-large. The ship's bridge, crew quarters and engines are all located in the stern, leaving nine-tenths of the ship to be taken up by oil container tanks.

CARGO STOWAGE

No other form of merchant ship is so devoted to cargo stowage as the tanker. Nine-tenths of a tanker consists of the carefully separated tanks holding the oil. A mere one-tenth of the ship holds the engines, crew accommodation, bridge and controls.

OIL SPILL

Supertanker accidents cause environmental ruin when the poisonous cargo floods into the sea. In 1989 an oil spill from the *Exxon Valdez* polluted 1,700 kilometres of coastline in Alaska. The tanker spilled 11 million gallons of oil, destroying local wildlife.

Lifeboat   Funnel   Bridge

GLOBTIK TO

FLOATING GIANTS

A supertanker simply dwarfs a big car ferry. Many supertankers are as long as four soccer pitches! The biggest, the *Jahre Viking*, is 485 metres long, 69 metres wide and weighs 565,000 tonnes. Not surprisingly, it is the world's largest ship.

Helicopter landing pad
Supplies are brought to the ship by helicopter.

Accommodation
The captain's and crew's living quarters occupy a tiny part of the ship.

Cargo pipelines
For pumping oil to shore.

Propeller
The five-blade screw propeller has a diameter of 9m.

Vertical and horizontal frames
Separate the oil into small compartments to prevent massive surging as the ship pitches and rolls.

The ULCC *Esso Atlantic* (1977) is 406m long and displaces 517,144 tonnes. Its 45,000hp steam-turbine powerplant is as high as a 16-storey building.

HIGH-TECH SAILING

Supertanker captains need great skill to pilot their huge vessels. Tankers have a wide turning circle and respond slowly to a change of course. Even at the low speed of eight knots, they need two kilometres or more to stop. On-board computers help navigation and reduce the risk of collision with other, smaller ships.

OFFSHORE PIPELINES

A fully laden supertanker lies too deep in the water – 22 metres or more – to enter an ordinary harbour. VLCCs and ULCCs use deep-water anchorages and unload their oil by pumping it through kilometres of pipeline to "tank farms" on shore.

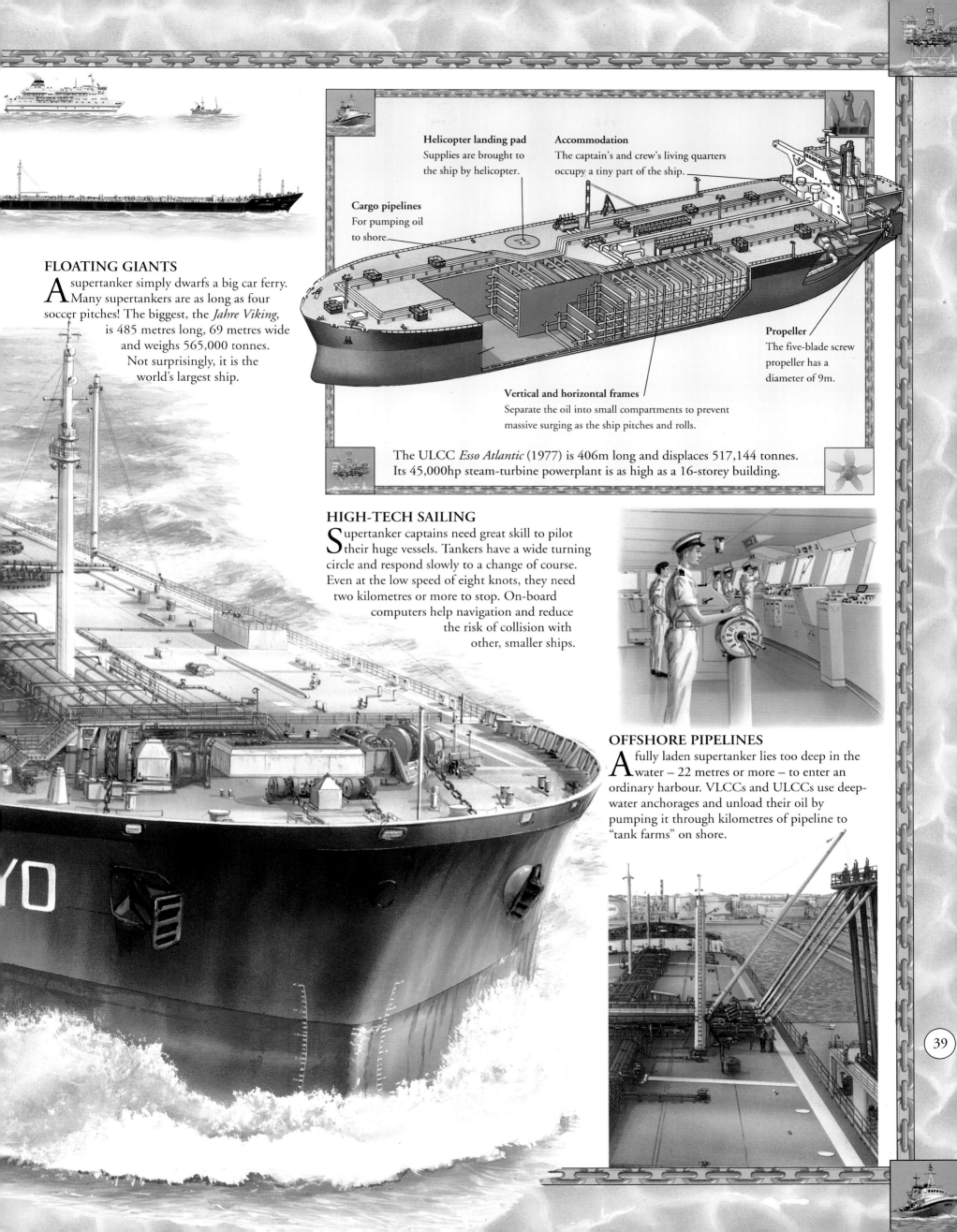

Destroyer

"After their Sea Dart SAM failed to fire, Glasgow held steady while we fought the battle. Two Sea Wolf SAMs were fired, and they took out the first two aircraft."
Captain John Coward, Falkland Islands, 1982

A hundred years ago, the first destroyers were light, fast warships designed to protect a fleet from torpedo attack. Then they were given tubes to allow them to make torpedo attacks themselves. Modern destroyers still have this dual role of defence and attack, but today their most important weapons are missiles. SSMs (surface-to-surface missiles) can attack other ships, and SAMs (surface-to-air missiles) can destroy aircraft.

Since World War 2, destroyers have also carried sonar and anti-submarine weapons. Modern destroyers carry helicopters to widen the search for submarines. A helicopter moves rapidly across the sea, using its sonar to detect enemy submarines. It uses its own anti-submarine weapons to attack the submarines. A destroyer like the French *Tourville*, shown below, has enormous fire-power and is very fast. It is armed with two 10-centimetre guns, Exocet SSMs, Crotale SAMs and Malafon hunting torpedoes. The ship's top speed is 34 knots.

RADAR

Modern destroyers have separate radar systems for detecting other ships and aircraft, for guiding missiles, and for navigating the ship.

MISSILE LAUNCH

Missiles are usually mounted in groups for rapid firing. French Crotale SAMs are mounted in two groups of four missiles.

AIR ATTACK RED!

Warship crews are not kept at battle stations all the time, but work at different levels of readiness. The most urgent level is "Air attack red". This means that an enemy missile or bomb attack might be only minutes or even seconds away. Anti-flash hoods and gloves reduce the risk of burns.

Radar array

SAM missile launcher

Helicopter landing pad

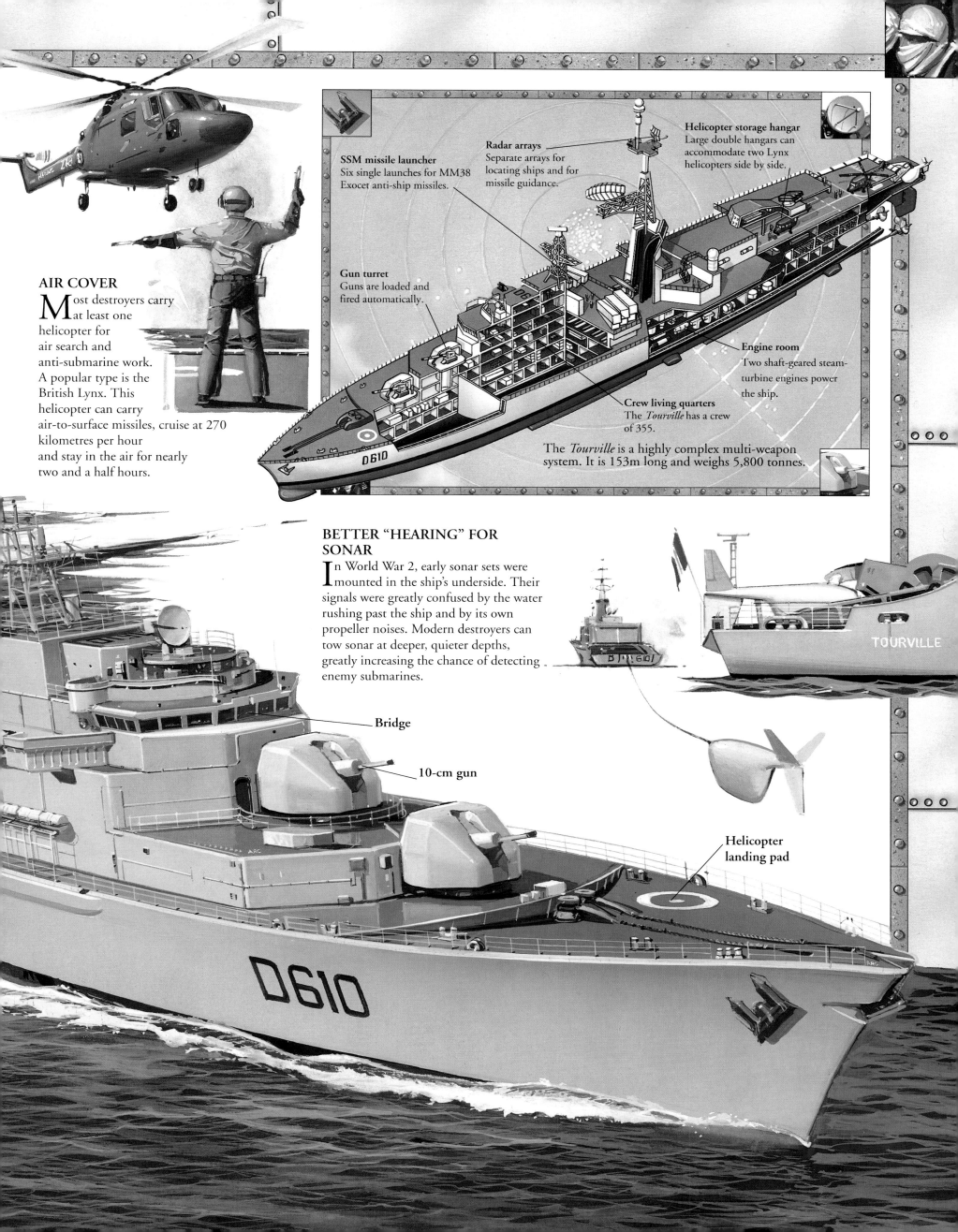

AIR COVER

Most destroyers carry at least one helicopter for air search and anti-submarine work. A popular type is the British Lynx. This helicopter can carry air-to-surface missiles, cruise at 270 kilometres per hour and stay in the air for nearly two and a half hours.

SSM missile launcher
Six single launches for MM38 Exocet anti-ship missiles.

Radar arrays
Separate arrays for locating ships and for missile guidance.

Helicopter storage hangar
Large double hangars can accommodate two Lynx helicopters side by side.

Gun turret
Guns are loaded and fired automatically.

Engine room
Two shaft-geared steam-turbine engines power the ship.

Crew living quarters
The *Tourville* has a crew of 355.

The *Tourville* is a highly complex multi-weapon system. It is 153m long and weighs 5,800 tonnes.

BETTER "HEARING" FOR SONAR

In World War 2, early sonar sets were mounted in the ship's underside. Their signals were greatly confused by the water rushing past the ship and by its own propeller noises. Modern destroyers can tow sonar at deeper, quieter depths, greatly increasing the chance of detecting enemy submarines.

Bridge

10-cm gun

Helicopter landing pad

TOURVILLE

D610

High-speed ferry

Over the past ten years, one of the most exciting new ship types to enter service has been the high-speed multi-hull ferry. The advantage of the multi-hull ship is that it is both light and stable, less likely to roll than a single-hulled ship and therefore more comfortable for passengers. A multi-hull, such as the *Hoverspeed Great Britain*, takes advantage of the fact that the less a hull is in contact with the water, the faster it will move through it. The *Hoverspeed Great Britain* features the wave-slicing bows of the old clipper sailing ship, and the lines of a modern powerboat, for extra speed. Unlike other craft, multi-hulls are driven by water-jet nozzles, two in each hull. Instead of having a rudder for steering, they are steered by pivoting the ends of the nozzles.

"BLUE RIBAND" AWARD

Before the high-speed craft of today, the fastest passenger ships afloat were giant liners competing for the "Blue Riband of the Atlantic", shown above. This trophy was awarded for the fastest Atlantic crossing.

WINNERS OF THE "BLUE RIBAND"

In June 1990 the world's biggest multi-hull, *Hoverspeed Great Britain*, crossed the Atlantic in three days, seven hours and 54 minutes. This broke the record of three days, ten hours and 40 minutes, which was set by the *United States* in 1952. The speed of the *Hoverspeed Great Britain* is compared, below, with the speeds of some of the previous winners.

1990 *Hoverspeed Great Britain* (36.65 knots)

1952 *United States* (35.59 knots)

1938 *Queen Mary* (31.6 knots)

1907 *Mauretania* (27.4 knots)

Bridge

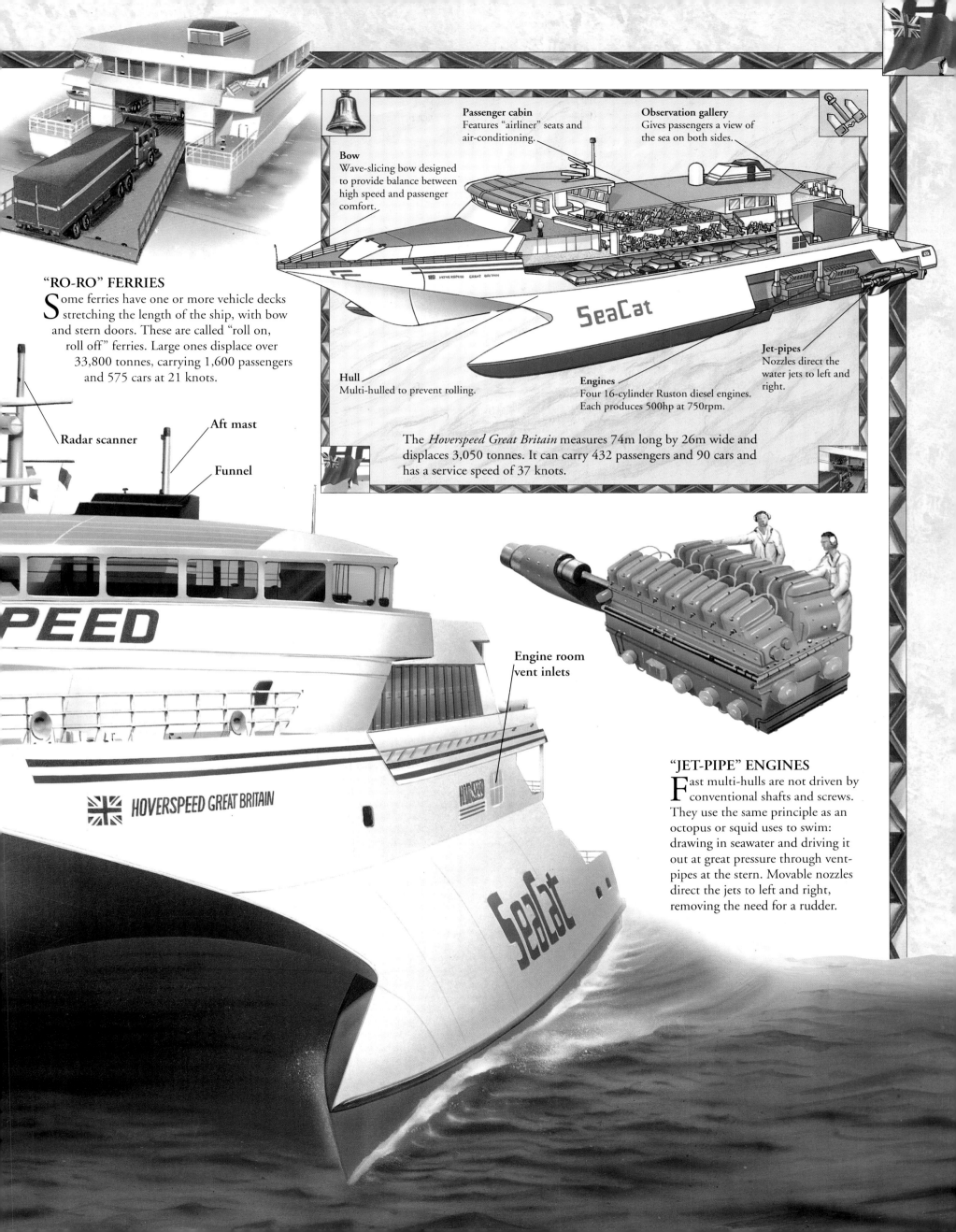

"RO-RO" FERRIES

Some ferries have one or more vehicle decks stretching the length of the ship, with bow and stern doors. These are called "roll on, roll off" ferries. Large ones displace over 33,800 tonnes, carrying 1,600 passengers and 575 cars at 21 knots.

Radar scanner

Aft mast

Funnel

Passenger cabin
Features "airliner" seats and air-conditioning.

Observation gallery
Gives passengers a view of the sea on both sides.

Bow
Wave-slicing bow designed to provide balance between high speed and passenger comfort.

Hull
Multi-hulled to prevent rolling.

Engines
Four 16-cylinder Ruston diesel engines. Each produces 500hp at 750rpm.

Jet-pipes
Nozzles direct the water jets to left and right.

The *Hoverspeed Great Britain* measures 74m long by 26m wide and displaces 3,050 tonnes. It can carry 432 passengers and 90 cars and has a service speed of 37 knots.

HOVERSPEED GREAT BRITAIN

Engine room vent inlets

"JET-PIPE" ENGINES

Fast multi-hulls are not driven by conventional shafts and screws. They use the same principle as an octopus or squid uses to swim: drawing in seawater and driving it out at great pressure through vent-pipes at the stern. Movable nozzles direct the jets to left and right, removing the need for a rudder.

GLOSSARY

aft
The word used to describe the rear section of a ship.

aircraft carrier
A heavy warship designed to operate aircraft at sea from its flight deck.

amidships
Steering the ship straight ahead.

anchor
A weight or large hook dropped on a cable to the seabed to stop a ship from drifting.

a-port
Steering the ship to the left.

artemon
An angled foremast carrying a spritsail. Used before the adoption of the bowsprit in the sixteenth century.

a-starboard
Steering the ship to the right.

ASW
"Anti-Submarine Warfare" or "Anti-Submarine Weapon": a depth charge, missile or hunting torpedo, used by surface ships against submarines.

ballast tanks
Tanks which can be flooded and emptied to make a submarine dive and surface.

battle-cruiser
A battleship with reduced armour to enable it to travel at greater speed.

battleship
A heavily armoured capital ship armed with guns which have bores greater than 22 centimetres in diameter.

beakhead
The pointed, enclosed space immediately in front of a sailing ship's forecastle.

beam
A ship's width from side to side.

belaying pin
Heavy wooden pin. Placed in racks around the sailing ship for securing the ropes.

bilge
Long, narrow plates on the lowest part of a ship inside the hull.

boom
A spar used to keep a sail stretched, support extra sails or carry anti-torpedo netting.

boum
A two-masted Arab sailing ship with lateen sails.

bowsprit
A large spar extended from a ship's bow to support stays for the foremast, and a boom from which jibs or a spritsail can be rigged.

bridge
A platform above the upper deck, from which a ship is controlled.

broadside
All the guns on one side of a ship, arranged to fire together.

bulkhead
A vertical wall dividing a ship's interior into separate compartments.

capital ship
The heaviest type of powered warship, usually describing a battleship, battle-cruiser or aircraft carrier.

capstan
A winch consisting of a cylindrical drum around which cables are wound. Used for heavy lifting work.

caravel
A small sailing ship of the fifteenth and early sixteenth centuries, capable of being rigged with either lateen or square sails.

carvel
A shipbuilding technique in which the planks of the outer hull are laid edge to edge.

castle
A structure built up from the bow and stern of a medieval sailing ship, from which soldiers could defend the ship and attack other ships.

catamaran
A multi-hull sailing craft or ship, consisting of two hulls joined by a central platform.

clinker
A shipbuilding technique in which the planks of the outer hull are laid with overlapping edges.

clipper
A high-speed sailing ship with a sharp, curved bow, designed to "clip" days off the journey time of other ships.

conning tower
The structure above the outer casing from which a submarine is commanded when on the surface of the water.

counterstern
A ship's stern which is high and curved, instead of square.

course
The largest, lowest sail supported by a ship's mast.

destroyer
A fast, light warship, originally intended to "destroy" enemy torpedo boats, with a combined surface, anti-submarine and anti-aircraft role.

dhow
Name for a lateen-rigged Arab sailing ship.

director
Control centre for directing the fire of a warship's guns.

displacement
The weight of a ship, measured by the tonnes of water displaced when the ship is afloat.

draught
The depth of water between the bottom of a ship's hull and the waterline when afloat, varying with the weight of its load.

dreadnought
A battleship designed to carry eight or more heavy guns, named after HMS *Dreadnought,* first of the type (1906).

figurehead
A painted statue mounted on a ship's bow, usually referring to the ship's name.

fore
The word used to describe the front, or forward, section of a ship.

forecastle (or fo'c'sle)
The space in the bow beneath a ship's short raised forward deck: traditionally the living quarters of the crew.

foremast
The mast of a sailing ship nearest to the bow.

frigate
A fast, light warship used to scout for the main battle fleet; nowadays mainly designed for ASW.

funnel
A large ventilator tube for carrying away the heat, smoke and fumes from a ship's furnaces and engines. Also called a smokestack.

galley
A ship's kitchen. Also a light, narrow warship driven by oars.

gun port
Square hole cut in a ship's side for a gun to fire through.

headwind
A wind blowing on to the bow of a ship, making progress difficult.

hull
The main body of a ship, consisting of the upper deck, the sides and the bottom.

island
The superstructure of an aircraft carrier, with bridge, funnels and masts, usually placed on the starboard side of the flight deck.

jib
A small triangular sail set between the foremast and the bowsprit.

junk
A Chinese sailing ship with three or more masts and matting sails stiffened with bamboo slats.

keel
A ship's backbone: the lowest and strongest timber or line of metal plates of the hull, stretching the full length of the ship's underside.

knot
A measurement of a ship's speed. A knot is the equivalent to one nautical mile, or 1.853 kilometres per hour.

lateen sail
A large triangular sail, rigged fore and aft instead of from side to side.

liner
A large, fast passenger ship belonging to the fleet of a shipping line.

mainmast
The tallest and strongest central mast of a sailing ship, between the foremast and the mizzenmast.

mast
A tall, vertical spar for carrying sails and, nowadays, radio and radar aerials.

mizzenmast
A sailing ship's rearmost mast, astern of the mainmast.

multi-hull
A ship designed for stability and speed, with more than one hull (two in a catamaran, three in a trimaran) joined above the water. Ferries are multi-hulled.

outrigger
A structure built outwards from a ship's side.

periscope
A long tube with viewing glasses, for seeing above the water's surface from inside a submerged submarine.

poopdeck
The shortest, uppermost deck of a ship, located at the stern.

propeller
A rotating screw, usually with two, three or four blades, which drives a steamship through the water.

quarterdeck
The upper deck of a ship, astern of the mainmast.

ram
A pointed, strengthened extension of the keel at the bow, for smashing and sinking enemy ships.

rigging
All ropes and cables used to support a ship's spars and to control the sails.

"ro-ro" ferry
A ferry designed for vehicles to "roll on" at one end of the ship and "roll off" at the other.

royal
A small sail, set above the topgallant.

rudder
A hinged flat timber or plate, hung from the sternpost and turned from side to side to change the ship's direction.

running rigging
All moving ropes and cables used to control a ship's sails.

SAM
A "Surface-to-Air Missile" for shooting down enemy aircraft.

ship of the line
A sailing battleship with two or more gun-decks, powerful enough to join the line of battle.

shrouds
The ropes or sails rigged from the sides of the ship to support the masts.

skysail
A small upper sail, set above the royal.

sonar
From "SOund NAvigation and Ranging". A device used for locating submerged submarines with pulses of sound.

spanker
A large four-sided sail. The lowest sail set from the mizzenmast.

spar
All pole supports used in a ship, including masts, yards and booms.

spritsail
A four-sided sail set from an artemon or bowsprit.

square rig
An arrangement of four-sided sails, set from yards running across the ship from side to side.

SSM
A "Surface-to-Surface Missile", fired at enemy ships.

standing rigging
All fixed ropes and cables that support a ship's spars.

stern
The back end of a ship.

studdingsail
A small extra sail, supported from a boom extended from the outer end of a yard.

submarine
A ship armed with tubes for firing torpedoes or missiles. It is able to dive, operate below, and return to the surface of the sea.

superstructure
The upper section of a powered ship, rising from the level of the top deck, including the bridge and funnel mountings.

tanker
A cargo ship designed to carry liquid cargoes such as crude or refined oil, or liquid gas.

tiller
The lever that turns the rudder from side to side.

topgallant
A sail set above the topsail.

topsail
A sail set above the course.

torpedo
A missile fired to sink an enemy ship by exploding beneath the waterline.

trimaran
A multi-hull sailing craft or powered ship, of three hulls joined by a central platform above the water.

trireme
A Greek war galley rowed by three levels, or banks, of oars.

U-boat
German term for a submarine, from *Unterseeboot*, meaning "under sea boat".

ULCC
"Ultra-Large Crude Carrier": used for supertankers of more than 300,000 tonnes displacement.

VLCC
"Very Large Crude Carrier": used for supertankers of 200,000-300,000 tonnes displacement.

yacht
A sail or powered vessel used for pleasure.

yard
A large spar hung from the mast, running across the ship from side to side, from which a sail is set.

INDEX